Léonard-Joseph-Marie Cros

The Heart of St. Gertrude

Or, a heart according to that of Jesus

Léonard-Joseph-Marie Cros

The Heart of St. Gertrude
Or, a heart according to that of Jesus

ISBN/EAN: 9783337318840

Printed in Europe, USA, Canada, Australia, Japan

Cover: Foto ©Lupo / pixelio.de

More available books at **www.hansebooks.com**

THE

HEART OF ST. GERTRUDE;

OR,

A Heart According to That of Jesus.

FROM THE FRENCH OF

LE PÈRE L. J. M. CROS, S. J.

BY P. P. S.

BALTIMORE:
JOHN MURPHY & CO.
1888.

SANCTO JOSEPHO
VIRO MARIÆ, DE QUA NATUS EST JESUS
CŒLITUM DECORI,
VITÆ NOSTRÆ SPEI CERTISSIMÆ
MUNDI COLUMINI.

Whenever St. Joseph's name was heard in Heaven, all the other Saints respectfully bowed their heads towards this Spouse of the Virgin Mother, and cast upon him looks of congratulation upon his incomparable dignity. (*Insinuation. Divin. Pietat.*, Lib. IV, Cap. xii.)

INTRODUCTORY.

IT has pleased our Lord to declare that the heart of St. Gertrude is a delightful abode for Him, and this revelation is confirmed by the following words of the Church in the Office for the Saint's Feast: "To manifest the merits of a Spouse so dear to Him, Jesus Christ has made known that He dwells in Gertrude's heart as in an abode of delight." The prayers for the Feast attest likewise, and in stronger terms, the Church's approbation: "O God," we read therein, "O God, Who hast prepared for Thyself in the heart of Gertrude a delightful abode, etc."

This heart being then in the eyes of the Church, a temple, a sanctuary, a tabernacle of Jesus Christ, Christian piety, far from being misled, is, on the contrary, assured of instruction and edification, in making it the object of an attentive study.

"But," some will say, "Jesus, the Heavenly Father, the Holy Spirit dwell in the hearts of all the Saints, in all hearts and souls filled with living charity, for so our Lord has declared; why then should the Church designate thus, in God's name, Gertrude's heart as an abode of Jesus Christ?"

Evidently, because Jesus Himself deigned to honor especially the heart of His spouse; for Gertrude is indeed privileged among the spouses of Jesus Christ.* To be convinced of this one needs but read the following words of the Heart of Jesus to Gertrude:

"I have chosen to dwell in thee, and find in thee My delight.†

---

* Sexaginta sunt reginæ ... et adolescentularum non est numerus: una est columba mea, perfecta mea. (Cant. VI, 7, 8.)

† Insin., L. I, Cap. xiv, xviii, edit. Salisburgens., 1662.

"In thee I wish to amass My treasures and collect all the riches of My grace; and if any desire and seek these goods, I will that they find them in thee.*

"I have made of thy heart a channel united to Mine, and through which waves of divine consolation shall flow into humble, confiding souls that seek it of thee.†

"Whatever a soul hopes to obtain through thy intercession, will surely be granted it.‡

"I wish to clothe Myself in thee: concealed under this protecting veil, My Hand may thus be enabled to seize sinners and do them good, without being wounded by their stings. I desire likewise to clothe thee in Myself, so as to communicate the same honors and favors to all whom thou wilt bring nigh to Me by recalling them to thy memory. ‖

"I attest upon My Omnipotence, that I

---

* Insin., L. I, Cap. xix.
† Ibid., L. III, Cap. lxvii.
‡ Ibid., L. I, Cap. xv, xvii.
‖ Ibid., L. III, Cap. xviii.

desire to take no complacency in any creature, without at the same time delighting Myself in thee. My love unites Me to thee by bonds so interlaced, that I will not live happy without thee.*

"Thou mayest give Me thy orders as if thou wert a queen, a sovereign: never was servant more prompt to obey his mistress's commands than I will be to comply with all thy desires."†

Such indeed, among many others of like import, are the words St. Gertrude herself declares she heard from the mouth of Jesus Christ. Hence, the following, also from our Lord, addressed to souls connected with Gertrude by a holy friendship, will not surprise the reader:

"One is ever assured of finding Me when seeking Me either in the Sacrament of the Altar, or in the soul and heart of My beloved spouse Gertrude.‡

---

* Insin., L. I, Cap. xii; L. III, Cap. v.
† Ibid., L. III, Cap. xxxiii.
‡ Ibid., L. I, Cap. iv.

"Her soul is so dear to Me that I have made it My refuge. And concealing Myself therein I find consolation for the outrages men heap upon Me.*

"She is all in all to Me: love has made Me her captive, and united her to Me even as the fire melts and fuses into one mass ingots of silver or gold.†

"She is a lily I love to hold in My Hand; she is My embalmed rose. ‡

"Gertrude's heart is as a safe bridge over which one may safely reach Me without falling or growing dizzy." ‖

Finally, a prayer of the Heart of Jesus to His Heavenly Father contains within itself and crowns all these praises:

"O Holy Father, for Thy eternal glory, may Gertrude's heart pour out upon men the treasures enclosed in My Human Heart." §

* Insin., L. I, Cap. iv.
† Ibid., L. I, Cap. iv.
‡ Ibid., L. I, Cap. iv.
‖ Ibid., L. I, Cap. xv.
§ Ibid., L. III, Cap. xxx.

Having heard these accents of the love of a God, one may no longer doubt that Gertrude's heart is a most privileged one, and Gertrude a spouse loved with an especial predilection. But what can be the secret of this predilection of Jesus Christ? The Church aids us to discover it, when she tells us that our Lord, before taking up His abode in Gertrude's heart, there *prepared* Himself a dwelling according to His desires; and Gertrude herself reveals the secret, laying open before us in detail the amorous industry of Jesus in fashioning her heart according to His own.

To study, to contemplate in the writings of St. Gertrude the common work of her soul and Jesus Christ's love,—is the object of this little book. No doubt, it will fall far short of what the author so earnestly desires it should be—a faithful portrayal of the spirit of the Saint, as evinced in the original; yet, in spite of this, he hopes his readers will find these pages both interesting and useful—interesting, because therein the heart of St. Gertrude is laid bare before them, and what Jesus so loved must needs be ever lovely and attractive—useful, because the lessons Jesus gave Gertrude are applicable to all Christians, and He will not fail to prepare for Himself a delightful abode in the hearts of all who hearken to His words with the avidity of Gertrude.

Moreover, it was for our instruction, and only in obedience to Jesus Who commanded her to do so, that Gertrude committed to writing these lessons of her Spouse.

"I could not," she says, "resolve to yield to our Lord's desires on this point; and one day He said to me: 'Thou shalt not leave this world until thou hast written what I desire thee to write. I exact this of thee, that these writings may be, in the far future, a pledge of My divine bounty ... through them will I benefit souls innumerable ... whilst thou writest, I will press thy heart to Mine, and instil into it, drop by drop, what thou shouldst say.'"

When the book was finished, Jesus appeared to her and said: "This book is Mine, and I have steeped it in the depths of My Heart; each letter has there imbibed the sweetness of My Divinity, and whoever, for My glory, shall read it with humble devotion, will derive therefrom the fruits of eternal salvation for his soul.

"For the salvation of mankind, I change, at the Mass, bread and wine into My Body and Blood: so, in like manner, have I consecrated this book by My benediction, that it may be conducive to the salvation of those who read it with humility and devotion.

"Not a letter in it but charms Me, for each exhales the ineffable sweetness of the perfume of My Mercy. This book is Mine, and I bless it; I adorn it with the roses of My Five Wounds, and I seal it with the Seven Gifts of the Holy Spirit, as so many seals attesting my possession of it, and no one shall be able to take it from Me."*

---

*Insin., L. II, Cap. x; L. V, Cap. xxxv. Vide alia, Cap. xxxvi et xxxvii.

Our Lord has given to St. Gertrude's book titles at once mysterious and explanatory. He calls it: Insinuations of the Divine Bounty, *Insinuationes Divinæ Pietatis;* Memorial of the Divine Bounty, *Memoriale Divinæ Pietatis;* Messenger of the Divine Bounty, *Legatus Divinæ Pietatis.* One readily perceives that this divine goodness pervading every page is the Heart of Jesus, so that the book is truly a *Messenger of the Heart of Jesus,* sent to souls to awaken in them the memory of His love and fill them with its divine influences.

Under the common title of *Insinuationes Divinæ Pietatis,* is published a volume in five books, the first and second of which were written by St. Gertrude's own hand, about the year 1289. The last three were only dictated by her, or written under her direction or by her orders, the irrefutable proof of which fact is found in chapter XXV, of the fifth book, where we read: " When this book was finished, Jesus appeared to her." Then follow the divine promises already referred to.

The Saint's secretary also gives us an account of the last moments and death of the Spouse of Jesus Christ.

The material of the present volume is taken principally from the first, second and third books of the Insinuations.

The first contains a biographical notice of St. Gertrude, and an abridged picture of her virtues. The author of this book was, for several years, the Saint's most intimate and confidential friend.*

In the second, St. Gertrude herself, and in the third, a depositary of her soul's secrets exposes the favors Jesus accorded her

---

*Ad (Dei) laudem, ea quæ multis annis secreta quadam familiaritate ab hac sancta virgine percipere potui, revelabo. (Lib. I, Cap. vi.) This confidant was perhaps the pious and learned Theodoric of Alpudia. Lanspergius says of him in his preface to the *Insinuationes:* "Qui cum sancta hac virgine varia saepenumero habebat colloquia, ejusque spiritum ac verba magnopere praedicabat. Quo etiam auctore liber natus est."

and the instructions He gave her in preparing her heart for the grace of perfect union.

We have borrowed from the fifth book the description therein given of St. Gertrude's happy end. All is delicious honey in Gertrude's book; and in reading it we are reminded of this counsel of the Holy Spirit: "It is not good for a man to eat much honey."

It had been easy indeed, were it necessary, to adduce pages of illustrious testimony in favor of the writings of a Saint whom Teresa of Jesus and Francis de Sales honored and loved as their spiritual mother, but the veneration the Church pays them renders their testimony all sufficient; and moreover, the Church herself declares that Gertrude was favored with divine revelations, and that her spiritual writings are wholesome food for Christian piety.*

---

* Office of the Saint, Lesson VI.—The holy abbot of Liesse, Louis de Blois, who lived about the year 1530, was accustomed to read over all St. Gertrude's

We shall make no effort to prove that in these marvellous communications between the Heart of Jesus Christ and Gertrude's, there is nothing that should be repugnant to the pious belief of the reader. This book is addressed to souls who value the judgment of the Church far above learned dissertation, and the Church recognizes that it has pleased Jesus to love thus His spouse Gertrude. Moreover, the lives of all the Saints reveal facts not less marvellous, and it is only the unthinking who are astonished that the God made man for love of man should thus deign to converse familiarly, in the present life, with those whose Brother He has become, and who are destined to a life of familiarity with Him in eternity.

writings twelve times a year; and he also advised those in whose spiritual advancement he was interested, to read them. The friend of his from whom we obtain this information adds: "The venerable abbot's writings are redolent of the spirit of St. Gertrude; there is scarcely a page of his precious works in which one cannot trace ideas evidently drawn from the source so dear to him."

THE HEART OF ST. GERTRUDE;

OR,

A Heart According to That of Jesus.

CHAPTER I.

Gertrude's Childhood.

THE illustrious order of St. Benedict has the honor of having given to the Church three virgin Saints named Gertrude.

The first was the daughter of the duke of Brabant, Pepin de Landen, and his virtuous wife, Iduberge. On becoming a widow, Iduberge founded the monastery of Nivelle, and there consecrated to God her daughter Gertrude, who died in the year 664, at the age of thirty-three.

Another Gertrude, daughter of Pepin the Short and Berbertha or Bertrade, died in the odor of sanctity, and was venerated after her death at the monastery of Neustadt, which Charlemagne, her brother, had founded. This blessed death occurred about the year 794.

But the most celebrated of the three Benedictine virgins is she whose memory the Roman Church honors on the 15th of November, and it is this Gertrude who forms the subject of our book.

Several centuries elapsed between her life and those of the other two. They who deny this could not certainly have read her writings attentively; for these give undeniable proofs that Gertrude devoutly celebrated the feasts of St. Bernard, St. Dominic, St. Francis—likewise, that she was not only a contemporary, and a friend of St. Mechtilde, but probably her sister.

Gertrude was born at Eisleben, in the Duchy of Mansfield, on the feast of the Epiphany, 1222. Her parents were noble and rich.

"In this blessed child," says an old historian, "the fruits seemed to precede the flowers; her first steps crushed under foot the vanities of the world, and her first salutation to it was an eternal adieu." And in reality she was not yet five years old, when with her parents' consent she retired to the monastery of Rodersdorff, in the diocese of Halberstadt.

Innocence was not the only virtue of the little Gertrude. Her good sense, prudence and piety were wonderful in one so young, and the amiability of her disposition was such as to win all hearts. To these qualities were added rare intellectual gifts, which with her love of study soon caused her to outstrip all her companions. At a very early age, she became familiar with the Latin language, and her fondness for literature amounted to a passion. Moreover, the purity of her heart permitted her to see clearly the true and beautiful, whilst the serenity that reigned in her soul could but favor in a remarkable degree her intellectual progress.

It was thus Gertrude grew from childhood to womanhood, preserved from even the shadow of evil, thanks to the continued vigilance of Him whose love ever encompassed her; and hence "it is Him we must thank, in Gertrude's name," says one who had her holiest confidence. May He be blessed throughout eternity! *

---

*Synopsis vitae S. Gertrudis, auctore Laurent. Clement. Benedictin.—*Insinuat.*, Lib. I, Cap. i.

CHAPTER II.

Gertrude's Conversion.

GERTRUDE had now reached her twenty-fifth year; her piety and many other beautiful qualities of mind and heart all combined to make her the ornament and treasure of the monastery of Heldelfs, when suddenly, enlightened from on high, she sees what no one else saw, and what hitherto had been unsuspected by herself— her soul was sterile, disordered, guilty even, and God invited her to be converted to Him.

I.

Let us listen to Gertrude's own account of this great event of her life:

"May my soul bless Thee, O God, my Creator! May all within me sing Thy praises! With what patient charity didst

Thou not shut Thy eyes, as it were, to the years of my infancy, childhood and youth, spent in the pursuit of vanity! For did I not indeed live as if a pagan among pagan people, ignoring Thee, my God, who dost reward the good and punish the wicked? Such was my folly that until I had nearly completed my twenty-fifth year, I would probably, without remorse or scruple, have permitted myself any thought, word or action, inconsiderate or even guilty, had not Thy mercy restrained me, either by increasing in my heart that natural horror of evil and relish for good so early implanted there, or by exciting the vigilance and zeal of the guardians of my soul.

"And yet, notwithstanding such conduct, what was there Thou hadst not done for me? When but in my fifth year, Thou didst introduce me into the sanctuary of the religious life, remitting me to the care of Thy dearest friends. Ah! should I not have spent every instant in blessing Thee! but alas! so negligent, so guilty indeed was my life, that, if possible, it had diminished Thy divine beatitude, and obscured that glory it should have been my most ardent desire to increase. Touched by Thy grace, my heart now deplores these wanderings, and Thou knowest, Thou alone knowest the bitterness of my regret."

It is but natural to ask, what then Gertrude's wanderings and errors were. Truth forces us to say that they were far other than those of sinners, being in reality nothing more serious than a certain juvenile levity, puerile vanities and an excessive love of study, literature and the sciences, as we shall soon learn from her own accusations against self.*

---

* All the Saints, even the most innocent, have regarded themselves as the greatest of sinners, which sentiment may be explained in several ways. We will content ourselves with giving but one explanation as contained in the following lines borrowed from the life of St. Francis of Assissium (Wading. annal.): "A companion of St. Francis said to him one day: 'Father, everybody runs after you and venerates you as a saint: now, tell me, what is

"Buried in an abyss of humiliation, I adore Thee, O Father of mercy, and praise Thy unbounded goodness; for this it was that when I walked in the paths of perdition ever bore me in mind, and meditated upon my soul, not indeed in designs of vengeance, but of love, seeking to exalt my baseness by the multitude and grandeur of its benefits, as if I had distinguished myself among men by the life of an Angel."

"It was in Advent, and on the next feast of the Epiphany I would complete my twenty-fifth year. Thou didst now fill my heart with an indescribable longing and unrest, whose salutary effects were to give me a disgust for the frivolities and levity of youth; this was the first step of Thy love

your opinion of yourself.' Francis replied, 'I am the vilest of sinners.' 'How can you think that?' was the answer; 'you are not a thief, a murderer, an adulterer.' 'If such sinners as you have mentioned,' said Francis, 'had received the graces I have, they would have made better use of them, serving God more zealously and advancing His glory far more than I have done.'"

in preparing my heart for Thyself. Then gradually, Thou didst overthrow the fortress of vanity and curiosity, which pride had raised in my interior, notwithstanding I bore the habit and name of a religious, alas, so unworthily!"

II.

"This unrest lasted until Monday, the 27th of the following January. That happy day saw an end to my puerile vanities, and the shades that had enveloped my soul were dissipated.

"The feast of the Purification of Thy chaste Mother approached. I was in the dormitory, after Compline, just at the beautiful hour of evening twilight, when one of our aged Sisters passed by. According to the rule of our Order, I made an inclination towards her in token of respect. Raising my head, whom should I behold but Thyself, O my Beloved, my Redeemer, O Most Beautiful among the children of men!

"Thou didst appear to me as an amiable, modest youth of about sixteen years of age, thus not disdaining to accommodate Thyself to my infirmities, in clothing Thyself with a form which Thou didst know would be pleasing to my eyes.

"Standing before me, Thou didst say to me in accents of indescribable sweetness: 'Thy salvation is near at hand; why dost thou so afflict thyself about it? Hast thou no counsellor, no friend who can assuage thy ever-renewed sorrows?'

"These were Thy words, and suddenly, though fully conscious that I was still in the dormitory, I beheld myself in the choir, in the corner where I was accustomed to make my careless, tepid meditations, and there Thou didst speak to me again: 'I will save thee and deliver thee; fear not,' Thou didst say, taking my right hand in Thy own noble hand, as if in pledge of Thy words, and adding: 'With My enemies thou hast licked the earth; suck now the honey sticking to the thorns; return to Me; I will welcome thee tenderly, and inebriate thee with the torrent of My divine joys.'

"Out of myself with excess of joy on hearing these words, I endeavored to approach Thee, but now saw, for the first time, that a long hedge, so long that I could see neither end of it, lay between Thee and me. I longed to force my way through, but it was bristling with sharp thorns, and in no part of it could I perceive the least break that would allow me to reach Thee, Thou only joy of my heart.

"And now, whilst burning with desire of reaching Thee, I detested and bewailed my sins and defects, of which this hedge was the figure; Thou, Father of the poor, didst extend Thy hand to mine, and immediately, without the least effort, I was beside Thee.

"My eyes fell upon Thy Hand, and there I saw, sweet Jesus, the scars of those Wounds that paid all our debts.

"And now, from this moment, my soul was enlightened, my heart softened, Thy powerful grace extinguishing within me all disorderly passion for worldly learning, and detaching me from all my vanities. What had heretofore charmed me, now appeared contemptible. I commenced to taste only Thyself, O my God. I had not known the interior of my soul; Thou didst acquaint me with it; and from this hour henceforth, in the depths of my heart, hast Thou conversed with me as a dear friend living under the same roof, as a tender Spouse with His Beloved.

"I praise Thee, I bless Thee, I return Thee thanks, not as I should, but as I am able, for having, with so much amiability and sweetness, commenced the work of my conversion. Blessed be Thy merciful wisdom which didst devise so engaging a manner of bringing under Thy yoke my stubborn, rebellious will, and making light and easy for me a burden I had believed insupportable."*

*Lib. I, Cap. ii; Lib. I, Cap. i; Lib. I, Cap. xxiii.—The Benedictine Father, Laurent Clement, fixes (and with some degree of probability) the

CHAPTER III.

Gertrude's Sanctification.

GERTRUDE'S heart was turned to God: the orators and poets of pagan Rome no longer charmed her ears and consumed her moments of leisure. She now devoted to the study of the Fathers of the Church and to meditation upon the Holy Scriptures, all the hours not allotted to prayer or the work of the Community. Very soon, mystic theology had no secrets from her; God taught her to penetrate the most hidden sense of the Inspired Books, and

period of Gertrude's birth in the year 1222. Hence, her conversion took place, January 27, 1247.—We lay especial stress upon these dates as important epochs in the life of our Saint. She herself furnishes us all the data and information, save that of one year.

she was enabled to instruct the clergy themselves, who often had recourse to her for enlightenment. Regarding herself as a depository of divine treasures, she felt constrained to dispense them to all around her; and not content with communicating to these alone, the lights which illumined her from Heaven, in the hours of study or prayer, she carefully preserved the memory of them in books written by her own hand, thus ensuring them to future generations.

Meanwhile, Jesus continued the work of sanctification which was to prepare for Himself a delightful abode in her heart. Jesus was working in and with Gertrude daily; but there are two especially memorable days which were characterized by such an abundance of marvellous graces that she has seen fit to mark the dates thereof: the eve of the Annunciation of our Lady, March 24, 1247, and the feast of the Ascension of the same year. She says:

I.

"Among the many graces received from Thee, O Light of my soul, from the hour of Thy first apparition, there is one that far outweighs all others. Heretofore I had never carefully considered the interior of my soul; but now my gaze was directed towards it, and illumined by Thee I discerned much therein that was intolerable to Thy sanctity; so great was the disorder reigning throughout that it were indeed an abode utterly unworthy of Thee. And yet my unsightliness repelled Thee not, my most loving Jesus; and in the frequent Communions of the days which followed, I saw Thee sensibly present, although not clear and distinct as in open day, but rather as if enveloped in auroral mists.

"Thou didst wish by this amiable condescension, to encourage me to continue the work which would prepare me for the full enjoyment of Thy presence and love.

"Scarcely had I set about this task, when

Thou didst deign to visit and fill me with the blessings of Thy sweetness—me, so unworthy of such favors. It was on a Sunday after Matins, and the eve of the Annunciation.

"How shall I describe the ineffable joys of Thy visit? I cannot find words to do so. I can but immolate, in the depths of my heart, a host of praise, conjuring Thee often to repeat this favor to myself and Thy elect, making us experience the sweetness of such union and joy as until that hour I had never imagined. Everything in my past life shows clearly that this was a gratuitous gift of Thy love.

"Thus didst Thou labor with marvellous suavity to detach my heart from everything and draw it to Thee.

II.

"Again, one day, in the interval between the feasts of the Resurrection and Ascension of our Lord, seated in the garden near a little lake, I let my thoughts revel in the beauties of the spot. I was charmed with the transparency of the waters, the refreshing coolness of the shade, the joyous flights of numberless birds, especially the doves, that flew hither and thither around me, but more than all, with the mysterious peacefulness of my retreat.

"It was then, O Jesus, Author of all true joys, Thou didst whisper to my soul: 'If, by gratitude, thou makest ascend to Me the waters of My graces; if, increasing in virtue, thou clothest thyself with good works like a rich verdure; if, detached from all earthly objects, thou art free like the dove to soar towards heaven, there to abide with Me, far from the noise of the world, thou preparest and givest Me a more delightful abode in thy heart than that of any garden, how beautiful soever it be.

"All day long, this thought was before me; and at night, kneeling to say the last prayers as usual before retiring, suddenly, my mind was filled with these words of the

Gospel: 'If any one love Me, he will keep My word, and My Father will love him, and we will come to him, and will make Our abode with him.' At the same instant, my heart of flesh, my corruptible heart felt that Thou hadst entered therein and taken possession of it, Thou, my God, my only Beloved!

"Oh! that my eyes could have shed an ocean of bloody tears to wash away the sink of iniquity within me, since Thou, O Sovereign Dignity, didst deign to make Thy abode with me! Oh! that I could, just for an hour, have snatched from my breast this heart, and rending it in pieces, cast it thus into a living brasier, that purified from the least stains, it might become not indeed worthy, but less unworthy of serving Thee as an abode!"

We have seen that Jesus draws Gertrude to Himself, contracts an alliance with her, and finally, establishes Himself in her heart. He must now fully assimilate that heart to His own, and consummate that union the perfection of which is expressed by St. Paul in these words: "I live, not now I, but Jesus Christ liveth in me."

New favors, of which the Saint has given us a detailed description, manifest in vivid colors these supernatural operations of grace. Gertrude mentions three of the principal ones: the impression of the Wounds of Jesus in her heart, which took place during the winter of 1249; the Transverberation of her heart, on the third Sunday of Advent, 1254; the transforming and deifying visit of the Infant Jesus to her heart, on the Christmas of the same year.

III.

"It was during the winter of the first, or perhaps the second year after my conversion, that I found in a little book, the following prayer.

"'O Lord Jesus Christ, Son of the living God, grant me to aspire after the possession of Thee; enkindle in my heart an ardent desire, a burning thirst for Thee. May I live and breathe in Thee, sweetest Jesus, and may all the pulsations of my heart, be directed to Thee, O Thou Supreme Happiness!

"'With Thy Precious Blood, most merciful Lord, engrave Thy Wounds upon my heart, that reading therein Thy sufferings and Thy love, I may be excited to compasate them, and the fire of ardent love for Thee, be enkindled within me. Grant that every creature may become as naught to me, and Thou alone my all.'

"This prayer pleased me very much, and I often recited it. It was during this same winter, soon after finding this little prayer, whilst seated in the refectory, near a Sister to whom I had confided the secret of several divine favors vouchsafed me, that I suddenly become conscious that our Lord, in spite of my unworthiness had deigned to hear me. I felt, O my God, that thou didst distinctly imprint upon my heart, the Stigmata of Thy Five Adorable Wounds; and notwithstanding my exceeding unworthiness, Thy infinite bounty, has, even to this hour, preserved therein the impression!

"Later on, in the seventh year of my conversion, towards the approach of Advent, a person, yielding to my importunity, daily recited before the crucifix the following short prayer for me:

"'O most loving Lord, I pray Thee by Thy wounded Heart to pierce Gertrude's with the arrows of Thy love, that being freed from all terrestrial dross, it may be thoroughly penetrated by the divine action.'

"Shortly after, on the third Sunday of Advent, during Mass, and especially as I was going to the altar, Thou didst enkindle in me, O my God, so ardent a desire for this favor that I was constrained to cry out, in the depths of my soul, 'Lord, I confess that I have done nothing to render myself worthy of the least of Thy gifts, and yet I dare conjure Thy bounty that regarding not mine, but the merits of souls here present, Thou wouldst deign to transpierce my heart with an arrow of Thy love.'

"I felt immediately that my prayer was answered. Having returned to my place, after receiving the Sacrament of Love, and casting my eyes upon the crucifix in the sanctuary, I saw escaping from the Wound in the Side a ray of light, pointed as an arrow.

"It inundated me with torrents of delight; but the desires of my soul were not fully satisfied until the following Wednesday.

"The Mass was nearly ended, the priest reading the words which recalled Thy adorable Incarnation. I was not altogether recollected and attentive, yet notwithstanding, it was then Thy arrow wounded my heart and Thou didst say to me: 'I will that the waves of thy affection rise to Me.'

"Thou, O God, Who readest all my secrets, knowest that Thy graces in my heart have always been as royal diamonds lost in an unclean vase. Oh! inspire then, him who reads these writings, with a tender compassion for Thee, that, admiring the bounty with which for the salvation of souls Thou hast consented to leave even until now Thy precious jewels in such a vile receptacle, and endeavoring to supply my deficiencies, he say to Thee with heart and lips:

"'O Father, O God from Whom all good proceeds, Thou dost merit all praise: to Thee be honor, benediction and glory!'

"It was the anniversary of that blessed night in which Heaven distilled upon earth the dew of the Divinity: whilst with my Sisters, exciting my soul to the holy offices of servant of the glorious Mother of the Infant Man God, I felt that a tender, new born Infant was placed in my heart. At the same instant, I beheld my soul entirely transformed; its color (if I may be permitted to call by the name of color, that to which nothing visible is comparable) was that of the infant; and I was filled with an ineffable comprehension of these **ravishing** words: ' God will be all in all.'

"Jesus now said to me: 'As I, in My Divinity, am the figure of the substance of My Father, so thou shalt be the living image of My Humanity; and as the sun communicates to the air, his own clearness and light, thus will I deify thy soul, penetrating it with the rays of My Divinity.'

"O power, O mercy of God! truly infinite indeed! how hast Thou poured the inappreciable liquor of Thy graces into a vase of clay, a vase destined of itself to ignominy!"

IV.

We have already observed, and St. Gertrude herself remarks it, that these marvelous favors and others with which she was honored, for instance, the interchange of hearts between Jesus and herself, conceal operations beyond the ken of human understanding. She designates them in her mystic language by such words as attraction, union, inhabitation, consummation. Nothing hinders our contemplating the image of that consummation in the scene just described, and no doubt it will be profitable for us to do so. The end of sanctity is indeed the being fully transformed into Jesus, and participating thus, in a measure incomprehensible, in the plenitude of the divine filiation. Now Jesus Himself in the Gospel, has given us clearly to understand, that the humility, sweetness and simplicity of His Heart, are just such as we see in childhood: for thus He expresses the perfection of sanctity when He says: "Whosoever, therefore, shall humble himself as this little child, he is the greater in the kingdom of Heaven." Hence, Jesus consummated this sanctifying work in Gertrude's heart, when under the form of the Infant God, He transformed it into the image of His Humanity, and inundated it with the rays of His Divine Nature.

Let us observe that these graces were not the work of sanctity, but rather successive compensations for work accomplished, and encouragement to new labors, these favors crowning virtues already obtained, and inviting Gertrude to the acquirement of others. The transformation which the Heart of Jesus wrought in Gertrude's progressed by slow degrees only, and it was not yet consummated, when nine years after her conversion, she exclaimed, "I have seen my heart transformed." And long years after, she still with Jesus pursued this grand work, striving earnestly to make her heart humble, sweet, pure, abandoned to God's good pleasure, and devoured with zeal for the salvation of souls,—in a word, a heart modelled upon that of Jesus.

Gertrude herself will reveal to us the labors that began and finally consummated its transformation, but she will first tell us how great a part the Blessed Virgin Mary had in this grand and beautiful work.

CHAPTER IV.

The Share the Blessed Virgin Had in Gertrude's Sanctification.

NO saint probably has understood better than Gertrude, the necessity and power of Mary's assistance in the sanctification of souls. Our Lord Himself was pleased to manifest to her the incomparable dignity to which the Blessed Trinity had exalted our Lady, making her co-operation essential and decisive in the execution of the divine plans.

I.

One day, whilst chanting at Matins the *Ave Maria*, Gertrude saw gush forth from the Heart of the Father, of the Son and of the Holy Ghost, three streams which penetrated to the Blessed Virgin's heart, and thence remounted to their source; whilst at the same time, she heard an interior voice saying in the depths of her soul, "After the power of the Father, the wisdom of the Son, the tender mercy of the Holy Spirit, nothing approaches the power, the wisdom, the tender mercy of Mary." And she was made understand, on the same occasion, that this effusion from the Heart of the Trinity takes place, every time a soul on earth devoutly repeats the *Ave Maria*; and it thus through the ministry of the Blessed Virgin, dispenses the dews of a new joy among the Saints and Angels, and itself receives an increase of those spiritual treasures with which the Incarnation of the Son of God had already enriched it.

It was indeed for love of Mary that God had pity on the human race, and communicated to it His divine riches, to participate in which man must first salute Mary. Gertrude, one day, heard Jesus say to His Mother, "It is for thy sake, O Queen, O Mother most loving, I have had pity on sinners." And again, Mary spoke thus to Gertrude. "In favor of those who recall to me the joy of my soul on the day of the Incarnation, I will realize the desires of the Church when she chants: "O show thyself a mother:" *Monstra te esse matrem*. Yes, I will show myself a Mother to them—Mother of the King of Glory and Mother of suppliant man—of the first, by displaying my power to assist,—of the second, by dilating for him the bowels of my compassion."

Gertrude had not always understood this double Maternity of the Blessed Virgin, and one Christmas day, whilst chanting the words: First-Born of the Virgin Mary: *Primogenitus Mariae Virginis*, she said within herself: "It seems to me that the title of Only Son were a far more fitting one for Jesus than First Born." But just then our Lady appeared and answered her thus: "No, not Only Son, but First Born is the fitting title; for after Jesus, my best loved Son, or rather I should say, truly in and by Him, I have engendered ye all in the bowels of my charity, and ye have become my sons, the brothers of Jesus."

II.

In the following manner, Mary deigned to make Gertrude understand yet more clearly the sovereignty she exercises over the Heart of Jesus in virtue of her Divine Maternity, and also her tenderness in still recognizing as the brothers of Jesus, souls even defiled by sin: She saw, one day, legions of angels giving their invincible protection to souls grouped around Mary: these were the Blessed Virgin's devoted servants—whilst to the shelter of her vast royal mantle which Mary spread out to cover them, ran multitudes of animals of every sort, which the glorious Queen of Heaven caressed with her hand, one after another: these were sinners yet stained by their sins; and the Blessed Virgin wished to show Gertrude by this, how she welcomes and protects them when they have recourse to her mercy, hoping it may lead them to repentance and reconciliation with God.

This Divine Mother manifested to Gertrude, on the Feast of His glorious Nativity, her maternal authority over the Heart of Jesus as follows:

Gertrude was saying the *Salve Regina*. When she came to these words: "*Turn then, most Gracious Advocate, thine eyes of mercy towards us*," she saw the Blessed Virgin holding the Divine Infant in her arms. Mary gently touched Him on the shoulder, and causing Him to turn His Face towards Gertrude and her companions: "Behold," said she, "'mine eyes of mercy'— they are those of my Son, Jesus, and I turn them upon all who invoke me, for their eternal salvation."

Jesus, on His side, revealed to Gertrude, in a thousand ways, the law He had imposed upon Himself of communicating His riches to man, only through the hands and Heart of Mary.

During one of the early days of her conversion, a conversion which was begun on the feast of our Lady's Purification, and signally blessed on that of the Annunciation, Jesus said to Gertrude, "I give thee My sweet Mother as thy Protectress, I confide thee to her care." When the hour of trial came, Gertrude terrified, called upon Jesus to help her. He replied: "I have given thee My own most merciful Mother for thine, and it is through her, I will dispense my graces to thee; have recourse to her in all thy necessities and thou wilt surely find strength and consolation."

Despite these reiterated lessons of Jesus Christ and our Lady, Gertrude could not, at first, banish an apprehension, alas! too common among Christians—she feared lest all these testimonies of respect, confidence and love for the Blessed Virgin might be prejudicial to the rights of her Divine Son; but He Himself gave her a new lesson on this subject which dissipated such scruples forever:

It was on the feast of the Annunciation. A priest in his instructions to the Community had so expatiated upon the virtues and grandeur of the Blessed Virgin, without mentioning the love of the Son of God in the Incarnation, that Gertrude felt worried and grieved. On returning from the sermon and passing an altar of our Lady, as usual she made an inclination before the statue, but with less warmth and devotion than formerly, directing her affections rather towards Jesus, the blessed fruit of the Virgin's womb, and proposing to herself this intention every time she henceforth saluted our Lady's image.

Very soon after, however, she felt troubled, and wondered within herself if she had not displeased the powerful Queen of Heaven. Then Jesus Himself in all condescension and sweetness answered her perplexities thus: "Never fear, dear daughter, to displease My Mother by directing all thy affections to Me; on the contrary, it pleases her. But to do away with thy scruples, henceforth, in passing her altar, devoutly salute her image and neglect Mine." "Oh!" replied Gertrude, "God grant I may never act thus! No, Lord, never could my heart consent to this! Art Thou not my Only Good, my Salvation, my Life? and shall I neglect Thee, to lay my tribute of love at the feet of another?" "My dear daughter," said Jesus gently, "obey Me, and every time thou thus neglectest Me to salute My Mother, I will experience the same joy and thou merit the same recompense, as if thou hadst cheerfully sacrificed immense gains to increase My glory."

Gertrude thus instructed, comprehended more clearly the Mystery of the Divine Mercy, which abandons the salvation of the world and the sanctification of souls, God's gifts, God Himself to the hands of a Woman, our Sister, our Mother; and she ever after, besought Mary's intercession with increased fidelity and ardor. That her Communions might be worthy and profitable, she always conjured Mary to prepare her for them; and Mary thus invoked, ornamented her daughter with the jewels of her own virtues, so that Jesus made known to Gertrude the joy of His Heart, at finding her radiant in the reflection of that beauty which alone, as sings the Church, could delight His gaze.*

If Gertrude's heart became thus a preferred abode of Jesus, it was only because Mary, listening to her prayers, prepared it for Him. One day at the hour of meditation, our Saint asked Jesus, "What can I do to please Thee yet more?" "Behold My Mother," was the answer, "endeavor to praise her worthily." Then Gertrude addressed Mary, as "the Paradise of delights," and congratulated her on having been chosen for the abode of her God, adding to these words of praise the following petition: "Obtain for me, I beg of thee, that my heart may be, in the eyes of God, adorned with such virtues as will cause Him

*Sola placuisti Domino Nostro Jesu Christo. (Office of the Blessed Virgin).

to deign select it for His dwelling." Mary testified that this prayer was agreeable to her, for it seemed to Gertrude that, at this same hour, the Blessed Virgin planted in her heart the roses of charity, the violets of humility—indeed, the various flowers of every virtue.

IV.

Soon, Gertrude's fears were no longer that she might honor our Lady too much, but too little. She felt the impossibility of ever herself paying the meed of respect and gratitude due this August Sovereign, this Universal Benefactress; and the Heart of Jesus alone, it seemed to her, was capable of supplying men's deficiencies in honoring and loving our Lady. We find frequent expressions of this sentiment throughout Gertrude's writings.

On the eve of one feast of the Assumption, deeply impressed with the thought that she had ever been sadly lacking in her duty towards the August Queen of Heaven,

Gertrude earnestly conjured our Lord Himself to make amends for her defects, and render His Mother favorable to her. Then Jesus, tenderly embracing His Mother, and with other demonstrations of filial love for her, addressed her in these words: "Deign, O most loving Mother, to look upon this soul I have chosen for Mine own, and regard it with not less tenderness than if it had always been most faithful and zealous in thy service."

Again, on the feast of Mary's Nativity, Gertrude with sighs and tears, accusing herself of her shortcomings towards our Queen, besought Jesus to repair her negligence, with this intention, reciting the *Salve Regina*, but offering it to Mary through the Heart of Jesus. Whilst thus engaged, she heard the most beautiful melodies arising from the Heart of Jesus to that of His Virgin Mother: it was a canticle of filial love with which He paid Gertrude's debts.

One time, as she was praying Jesus to present His Mother some good works in her name, thus to repair the little zeal she had heretofore manifested for the Blessed Virgin's glory, Jesus, the King of Glory, arose, and offering Mary His Divine Heart, said: "Most loving Mother, behold My Heart: I offer it to thee with all that divine and eternal love which prompted Me to predestinate, create, sanctify and choose thee for My Mother. I offer thee in this Heart all that filial tenderness, of which I gave thee so many tokens on earth, when thou didst nourish and bear Me, a little child in thy arms. I offer thee, in this Heart, that faithful love which kept Me near thee all My mortal life, obedient to thy wishes, as any other son to his mother—Me, the King of Heaven. I offer thee especially, that love which on the Cross, made Me, in a measure, forget My tortures to compassionate thy bitter desolation, and leave thee in My place, a guardian and son. And lastly, behold in My Heart, the love which prompted Me to exalt thee in thy blessed Assumption, far above the

Saints and Angels, and crown thee Queen of earth and Heaven. All this I offer thee, dearest Mother, to supply the negligencies of my beloved in thy service, and I entreat thee at the hour of her death to meet her with a mother's welcome."

"O my Brother," said our Saint on another occasion to Jesus Christ, "O my Brother, since Thou hast been made Man to pay man's debts, deign now, I pray Thee, to supply the deficiencies of my indigence, and make amends for my negligencies in Thy Blessed Mother's service."

Jesus immediately arose, and advancing respectfully towards His Mother, fell upon His knees, and saluted her, bowing His head with a dignity and grace incomparable.*

* Ad quae verba Filius Dei, reverendissime assurgens et procedens, coram Matre sua genua flexit, et motu capitis eam decentissime et amicabilissime salutavit.

V.

In thus answering Gertrude's prayers, our Lord gave her, as we perceive, lessons of ever increasing respect and affection for our Lady, from which the Saint learned how impotent were all man's efforts to honor Mary worthily did not the Heart of Jesus Itself pay our debts. How indeed could man ever sufficiently revere her before whom the Son of God deigned to bend the knee? Gertrude, at last, comprehended something of the unsearchable depths of those words of the Gospel declaring that Jesus was *subject* to Mary, and henceforth called her the Sovereign, the Lady of the Heart of Jesus.*

* The title of Sovereign of the Heart of Jesus is indeed the grandest of the glorious ones bestowed upon Mary; for all the treasures of the Divinity are contained in the Heart of Jesus, and the Holy Trinity Itself, finds therein Its highest Heaven. Hence, we cannot call upon her too often by this sweet and glorious title, our Lady of the Heart of Jesus. Devotion to Mary under this title was

One more incident in Gertrude's life will finish the instructions of this chapter, and teach our readers an easy means of drawing down upon themselves and others our Lady's most abundant benedictions:

As Gertrude was praying one day, the Blessed Virgin was shown to her under the figure of a dazzling white lily, before the Holy Trinity. This lily had three leaves, one representing the power of the Father, one, the wisdom of the Son, and a third, the benignity of the Holy Spirit, which each of these Divine Persons had communicated to her in such a degree as to reproduce in her their vivid resemblance.

The Blessed Virgin now said to Gertrude: "If any one salute me devoutly as the white Lily of the Trinity, the brilliant

established at Paray-le-Monial, the source of devotion to the Heart of Jesus, and in the year 1846, that of the coronation of Pius IX.

We leave our readers to imagine the incomparable grandeur to which God was pleased to raise the Blessed Virgin's Spouse, St. Joseph, when He deigned to make His Son *subject* to Him.

Rose of Paradise, I will do for him what I can through the omnipotence of the Father, the wisdom of the Son communicated to me for the salvation of man, and the superabundant mercy which, flowing from the benignity of the Holy Spirit, fills my heart; and at the hour the soul which shall have thus saluted me, quits the body, I will appear to it in the splendor of such beauty, as will be to it a foretaste of the joys of Paradise."

From that day, Gertrude took the resolution of addressing our Lady or reciting before her image the following salutation:

"I salute thee, White Lily of the glorious and ever peaceful Trinity, brilliant Rose of Paradise. O thou of whom the King of Heaven was born, and with whose milk He was fed, nourish our souls, I entreat thee, with thy divine graces."*

---

*Ave, candidum lilium fulgidae semperque tranquillae Trinitatis, Rosaque praefulgida cœlicœ amœnitatis, de qua nasci et de cujus lacte pasci Rex cœlorum voluit: divinis influxionibus animas nostras pasce.

CHAPTER V.

The Humility of Gertrude's Heart.

WE have seen that the Blessed Virgin prepared Gertrude's heart for Jesus by sowing it thick with violets. From Gertrude's heart indeed, as from that of Jesus, arises the perfume of humility, and all her words are redolent of it.

"O God of my life," she writes, "what desert places, what rough and rocky roads hast Thou not been forced to traverse—I mean, what resistance of will had not Thy grace to surmount, ere reaching the valley of my misery!

"Whence comes it, O my God, that Thou dost humiliate Thyself thus, even to lavishing upon me the gifts of Thy bounty? Perhaps Thou wishest to make a trial in me of the truth of these words of St. Bernard:

'Thou pursuest those who fly from Thee; Thou seekest the face of those who have already turned their back upon Thee; Thou implorest, and they continue to despise Thee, yet nothing can repel Thee, nor diminish Thy love!'

"O superabundant sweetness of my God! I see that my sins, my multiplied crimes, grieve more than they irritate Thee! Truly, to bear thus with my miseries, Thou must needs have, it seems to me, greater treasures of benignity and patience than when in those days of Thy life on earth, Thou didst so tenderly bear with the company of the traitor Judas.

"Thou knowest, O my God, wherefore I am overcome with sorrow and confusion—it is because of my infidelity, my negligence, my irreverence, my ingratitude for Thy benefits. Yes, hadst Thou given me but a bit of twine, me so unworthy of anything, it should have merited more reverence and love than I have returned Thee for all Thy graces.

"O my God, where is Thy wisdom? What strange love has thus made Thee forget Thy dignity? What intoxication, if I may dare use the expression, has possessed Thee, that Thou seekest in the depths of its baseness so vile a creature as I, to unite Thyself to it? Ah! Thou wishest to teach men confidence in Thy love, for nowhere couldst Thou find one who shows less appreciation of Thy gifts, and scandalizes his brethren more."

Every page of Gertrude's book is filled with such expressions; and often, even more merciless than this against herself, she descends into such abysses of humility that we are not able to glance at their depths.

II.

By act, not less forcibly than word, did Gertrude manifest the humility of her heart.

"Abbess of the monastery for forty years," writes one of her companions, "she was most faithful in her attentions to the infirm, recreating with them as a mother with her children, and never hesitating to perform the lowest and most menial offices for them. She was first to sweep the house; and for a long time, this part of the manual work she did entirely, until the example of her humility had vanquished the repugnance of the Sisters to share it."

The author of the first book of the *Insinuationes* furnishes yet more decisive proofs of Gertrude's humility in the following: "She whom the wisest consulted, she so versed in the knowledge of Scripture, consulted the opinion of others in all things, being ever ready to follow or suspend, or abandon her own desires and plans according to the approval or disapproval of those to whom she submitted them. It was but seldom indeed she judged it her duty to prefer her own opinion to that of others, and she acted in such cases very reluctantly.

"Gertrude did not conceal the graces she

received from God; on the contrary, as we have already seen, she loved to communicate them not only to the directors of her soul, but to others, and this from a principle of the purest humility. Fully penetrated with the sentiment of her utter unworthiness of such favors, she did not doubt that they were lavished upon her only as precious seeds to be sown in better soil. It was dishonoring these gifts of God, she thought, to leave them buried in the mire of her own heart, and they would not begin to fructify for their Master until they were drawn forth, and deposited in another more worthy of receiving them."

Hence, the zeal with which she wrote and dictated the last four books of the *Insinuationes* and other works not now extant. At first, natural instinct and a humility not uncommon, made her shrink from it, but a more perfect humility triumphed, and she pursued these labors with a view solely to God's honor and glory, and her neighbor's salvation. Having finished these books, she would often say: "If, after death, I am cast into hell for my sins, there will remain for me one consolation—the thought that others, reading my writings, will praise God, and His graces, sterile in me, will bring forth in them, blessed fruits of immortality"—words embalmed in the perfume of humility and charity.

One of the industries of Gertrude's humility was not to struggle directly against the imaginations of pride or vanity. Did such thoughts strive to penetrate her meditations or mingle with her good works, she would immediately say to herself: "Yes, it is true that, in addition to all my other miseries and defects, I must also bewail pride, yet one consolation remains to me: perhaps others in witnessing my good actions will be led to imitate them, without imitating my pride, and thus God will be glorified and gather at least this fruit from my sterility."

III.

Gertrude's humility was not the sudden growth of a day; the generous virgin had acquired this virtue only at the cost of daily struggles, guided and sustained therein by the lessons of Jesus Christ.

Jesus left Gertrude some spiritual infirmities as the safeguard of her humility.

A pious woman, yielding to Gertrude's entreaties, had been praying for her some time, when one day, our Lord said to her: "These defects over which My Beloved grieves are very profitable to her. I daily fill her soul with such an abundance of graces, that, to preserve her from the attacks of vanity (for she is human), I must needs conceal some of them from her under the cloud of these trifling defects. Manure fertilizes the earth: the soul's consciousness of her failings evokes acknowledgment, and every time she thus humbles herself for them, I bestow upon her a new grace which destroys them; little by little, I change them into virtues, until the soul, one day, finds herself in an atmosphere of unclouded light."

Sometimes, Jesus would deprive Gertrude of these favors. His reasons for this He made known to her as follows: "It is for the sanctification of thy soul, I elevate thee by contemplation, to the knowledge of My divine secret; and in like manner, for thy salvation, do I exclude thee from them. When elevating, I wish to teach thee, that with the assistance of My grace, thou canst comprehend and accomplish great things; and abasing thee, the lesson to be derived therefrom is thy nothingness apart from Me."

Jesus showed Gertrude how He alone, as St. Paul tells us, is all sufficient—that we must remain in Him and be clothed with Him if we wish to please God.

Holding His Heart in His hands one day, He presented it to Gertrude, saying: "Behold, My Heart, that harmonious Instrument whose sweet tones ravish the Holy

Trinity. I give It to thee that, like a faithful, zealous servant obedient to thy commands, It may supply thy deficiencies. Make use of It, and all thy works will charm God's ear."

Gertrude hesitated, but Jesus triumphed over her fears, enlightening her humility by the following simile:

"A man," said He, "is called upon to sing before an honored assembly, but his voice is so weak and false that it pains one to hear it. Thou art near him, thou whose voice is clear, flexible, and sweet. Thou offerest either to lend him thy voice (which thou canst do) or sing in his place. Wouldst thou not feel indignant if he refused thy generous offer? And thus is it with thee and Me. I know thy poverty, thy deficiencies, and My Heart ardently desires to supply them—this were Its greatest joy. It asks only of thee that thou give thy consent, if not in words, at least, by a sign."

To make Gertrude understand that God finds not in us, but in Himself, the impulses of His bounty, Jesus gave her a new lesson on this important truth in which humility strikes its deepest roots:

One day, enlightened from above, Gertrude discovered in her soul some defects hitherto unperceived. "Lord, Lord," she exclaimed, horrified at the sight of her spiritual deformities, "how could I ever have pleased Thee with so many stains on my soul? and how many more may there not be upon it which none but Thine All Seeing Eye can discern!" Immediately she heard these words: "Love makes complacency," which she understood thus—"Love, even among men, so governs the heart as to render attractive and pleasing the object beloved, though it be unsightly and deformed—it sometimes carries one to the point of wishing to share these defects, as if they were not blemishes but the opposite. Now God is love itself, and in this lies the secret of His loving us, despite our spiritual deformities."

Jesus also gave Gertrude another shield

against the assaults of pride, by telling her the reason of the very especial favors He seemed to reserve for her:

"It was a feast-day," writes our Saint; "not being able to communicate on account of sickness, I refreshed my soul by calling to mind the benefits of my God. The contemplation of the many and great graces I had received, made me fear lest the wind of pride, passing over my soul, should dry up the dews of mercy; and I begged our Lord to give me some especial antidote against vanity, and here is the lesson of His paternal goodness:

"'In a large family of children, strong, healthy, and handsome, will always be found one lacking these qualities—delicate, homely, and otherwise unattractive perhaps. Is not this the child towards whom the father's heart goes out with most tenderness and compassion, which he expresses in little presents and caresses denied the others?'

"Jesus also said to me, 'As long as thou continuest to consider thyself the most imperfect, so long will I inundate thy soul with the waves of My divine tenderness.'"

IV.

Jesus gave Gertrude still other lessons on this same subject—humility. She learned from Him that pride closes the doors of the soul against grace, whilst humility opens them and introduces it therein.

She was once praying for a person who greatly desired to taste divine consolations. Jesus appeared to her and said: "This soul has no one to blame but herself that the sweetness of My grace cannot reach her— she is too full of herself, attached to her own ideas, obstinate in her judgments. The effect of such pride in the soul is to paralyze that faculty which inhales the perfume of divine love. Vainly indeed were sweet odors exhaled near a person, whose nostrils were so obstructed that he could not perceive them."

Again, as she was praying for another who had been recommended to her, both directly and indirectly with the deepest humility, she saw Jesus incline towards that soul, with ineffable condescension, inundate it with celestial splendor, and fill it with the graces it had hoped to obtain through Gertrude's intercession. At the same time, He said to our Saint: "Humility is so dear to Me, that when a soul humbly recommends itself to the prayers of another, hoping to obtain My grace through such intercession, I will never fail to grant its desires, even though the person asked to pray may never have done so."

Gertrude was once so overcome at the consideration of the magnitude and number of her sins (for such was the picture of them upon her delicate conscience) that she wished to flee the light and lose herself in an abyss of darkness. But whilst thus humbling herself, she saw Jesus descending towards her with such demonstrations of love that the Angels and Saints were filled with admiration. And Jesus, as if answering their astonishment, said: "I can but follow her; her humility has captivated My Heart and drawn It to her by bonds I cannot break."

But perhaps the most efficacious of all the lessons on humility Jesus gave Gertrude, was to be found in the divine delicacy with which He treated her. Often He seemed blind to those defects His Spouse bewailed, and the more her noble heart deplored them, the greater His apparent ignorance of them. The following incident will reveal the exceeding delicacy and sweetness of the love of Jesus in His dealings with Gertrude:

"O my Master," exclaimed our Saint on one occasion, "Thou dost work no greater miracle than this—that the earth supports me—me, an unworthy sinner!" "Yes," replied Jesus immediately; "cheerfully indeed should earth offer to bear thy footsteps, since Heaven itself with inexpressible impatience, awaits the happy hour when thou wilt tread its precincts!"

CHAPTER VI.

The Benignity of Gertrude's Heart.

JESUS is as kind and gentle as He is humble—says the Apostle of the Gentiles, "the goodness and kindness of God our Saviour appeared."* Hence, Gertrude's heart to please Jesus, must reproduce the benignity that filled His own.

The lessons of this gentle Master warned her against the shoals of anger, irritation and rancor; and sinners' iniquities, or the imperfections of the just, viewed in the light of these divine instructions, excited not indignation, but pity. She knew how to reprove without harshness, and overflowing with that charity imbibed from the Heart of Jesus, she was disposed to do

---

*Benignitas et humanitas apparuit Salvatoris nostri Dei. (Tit. III, 4).

or suffer anything that could aid or console her neighbor.

As she was praying one day for some wretches who had not only already heaped injuries upon the Community, but threatened still more, our Lord appeared to her. Showing her His Arm painfully twisted and bent, He said: "Consider what excruciating pain anyone would cause Me, who should strike heavy and repeated blows upon this Arm. And yet this is just what they do who breathe out resentment and fury against the people who persecute thee, forgetful of the fact that these wretches imperiling their souls thus, are still members of My Body. They, on the contrary, who pray Me to touch thy persecutors' hearts and convert them, who gently exhort them to repair their wrongs, are to Me, like skilful physicians, who pouring over My Arm with gentle hand, a healing oil, gradually and painlessly bring back the muscles to their right position."*

---

* The reader must ever bear in mind that, as St.

Surprised at this excess of divine benignity, Gertrude replied: "Dear Lord, how canst Thou call such unworthy people Thy Arm?" "I call them thus in all truth, because they are part of the Body of the Church, of which I am the honored Head." "But are they not cut off from the Church, by solemn excommunication, for their lawlessness?" "Yes, it is true they are excommunicated; but as they may yet receive the Church's absolution should they repent, I consider this a bond uniting them to Me, and the interest of their souls causes Me inexpressible solicitude. Oh! how ardently I desire their conversion!"

Gertrude begged Jesus to protect the convent from the evils with which these wretches threatened it. "I will do so," replied our Lord, "if, in humility of heart,

---

Paul says, the Church is the Mystical Body of Jesus Christ, and we, the members. Jesus speaks of the Wounds of His Mystical Body. It was in this same sense, He could say to St. Paul himself: "Why persecutest thou Me?" when Saul was 'breathing out slaughter' against the Christians.

thou acknowledge that these chastisements of My paternal bounty, are merited; if, on the contrary, thy pride fill thee with wrath against these unhappy creatures, by a just judgment, I will allow them to prevail and do thee still greater injury."

Whilst Gertrude was once praying for a very imperfect soul, she beheld Jesus, the right side of His Body arrayed in royal vestments, whilst the left exposed to view was full of ulcers. It was made known to her that the former represented souls advanced in virtue; the latter, those who were still very imperfect—also, that to pray for the former is to clothe Jesus in costly apparel; whilst to criticise the imperfect, or harshly reproach them for their faults, their spiritual miseries, is furiously to tear open the ulcers of Jesus Christ.

Such was the interpretation our Lord gave His Spouse of this vision, saying moreover: "Would to God my friends would strive to heal the wounds of My Church which are Mine own, by bearing with and healing the defects of the imperfect. Sores should be handled very carefully; likewise, should one treat gently the soul whose defects it hopes to cure, having recourse to severity, only when assured that no other means will effect the desired reformation."

II.

"How many," continued Jesus, "have no compassion for My wounds! Seeing their neighbors' faults, they immediately take advantage of it to bring them into contempt, instead of kindly giving a salutary word of correction, afraid lest the latter course might expose themselves to disagreeables, or be too much trouble; and their excuse for this neglect of duty is that of Cain: 'Am I my brother's keeper?' These are they who spread an ointment over My ulcers that inflames them and breeds worms in them. A word in season, perhaps, had corrected their brother's faults; whilst ill-timed silence and oblivion of them is often nourishing food to their growth.

"Others, indeed, inform the Superiors of their brethren's defects, but they are so indignant that the correction is much less grave than they expected, that they take the resolution of never again making known these matters to Superiors who apparently deem them so trifling. At the same time, they sit in judgment, harsh judgment upon the unhappy ones, the cure of whose spiritual infirmities they profess to have at heart, and never address them one kind word calculated to direct their steps aright. These also spread an ointment upon My sores, but under it is concealed their hypocritical hand, holding a sharp-edged trident which rends and tears them.

"Others again, who could correct their neighbor, neglect it, not from malice, but indifference; and these cause me the same pain as if passing near Me, they crushed My feet under their own.

"Some strive to correct, but in doing so,

neglect three very important rules of efficacious correction—first, that he who corrects, prepare himself for it by serenity of countenance, charity in words, and delicacy of action; secondly, that he observe secrecy regarding the faults committed, or, reveal them only to those who should know them, either to aid in the correction, or withdraw from the influence of bad example; thirdly, that he act promptly when the favorable moment for correction arrives, laying aside all human respect, all timidity, and having in view solely God's glory and the salvation of souls.

"One must know how to close his eyes to light failings. How often does it not happen that little children dispute among themselves when playing? A certain animation seems to fire every one of them, but it is not wrath; and the good father who witnesses their spirited contentions will most frequently be blind to them. Yet his conduct would change should one of the children get angry and threaten, or even strike another. And thus do I daily dissimulate, in regard to the trifling contentions of my children—I, the Father of Mercies; and, nevertheless, I prefer peace, perfect harmony."

III.

All who knew Gertrude attest that her conduct was regulated upon these lessons of Jesus Christ, and that the most hardened hearts yielded to her influence, her kindness, according to the Evangelic Words, gaining an absolute empire over wills the most rebellious.*

Gentle and affectionate towards the wicked, Gertrude lavished upon her companions a love truly maternal; and our

---

* Gertrude never saw suffering without being touched by it; the sight of a wounded bird, or a beast of burden struggling under a load beyond its strength, always appealed to her heart, and when unable to assist them in any way herself, she had recourse to God, begging that He would aid His poor creatures.

Lord, to excite her zeal for charity, made known to her, by the following incident, the value of any work, no matter how insignificant, if inspired by fraternal charity:

In spite of her infirmities, Gertrude had arisen one day to recite Matins, and had already finished one Nocturn, when another sick Sister took a place near her. Our Saint offered to begin again, and, with great devotion repeated what she had already recited. Mass followed, and during it, Gertrude suddenly saw herself arrayed in a mantle glittering with diamonds. Jesus had recompensed her charity for the sick religious, and the mantle had as many diamonds as the Nocturn contained words.

The sight of this exterior decoration revived in Gertrude's heart the sentiment of her unworthiness; she bethought herself of several faults she had not been able to make known to the confessor, then distant from the monastery; and grieved at not having it in her power to accuse herself of them before receiving Holy Communion.

"Why," said Jesus, "dost thou worry so over these faults, when thou art enveloped in this rich mantle of charity? Dost thou not know that charity effaces all thy sins?" "And have not these faults left their stains upon my soul?" "No," was our Lord's answer, "charity has not only effaced the faults, but also their stains; not so thoroughly does the sun penetrate and illumine crystal, as charity the soul, making it resplendent with the treasures of new merits."

CHAPTER VII.

The Purity of Gertrude's Heart.

SAID a holy old man to whom Gertrude manifested all the secrets of her soul: "I have never known any one more a stranger than Gertrude to aught that might wound chastity or obscure its brightness."

I.

Gertrude wished to please the most innocent Heart of Jesus; and she took great pains to preserve the lily of her virginity in all its whiteness and fragrance. Those who were best acquainted with her, attest that she never looked upon a man's face, so that by the countenance alone she could never have recognized even those who visited her most frequently.

Though passionately fond of reading the Scriptures, if she came upon a line, or a word, that seemed not written for her, she would instantly turn away her eyes.

To the delicate questions often addressed her by souls tormented by importunate temptations, Gertrude would reply with wisdom and charity; but it was easy to see that she had rather have been pierced by a sword, than add one useless word to these necessary conversations.

II.

It was of a purity whose roots were far-reaching and deep that Gertrude showed herself jealous, for God is jealous of it—that which strives to destroy in the heart the germs of its least faults—that which keeps the heart detached from all purely natural friendship, all material possessions, all useless solicitude, permitting it to seek in everything but God alone. The following will enable us to understand more clearly this perfect purity of Gertrude's heart:

She detested as a mortal poison all friendships not founded upon charity or thoroughly imbued with it. A word, a sign of affection, when she perceived the purely human tenderness inspiring it became insupportable to her. Few could appreciate like herself the sweetness of friendship; and her continual tribulations and trials urged her to those outpourings of the heart which are so great a relief; yet she preferred the renunciation of such consolations, rather than be the object of a friendship cemented by nature only, or the occasion of one affectionate word not ennobled by charity. Kind and charitable to all, she was very careful to address none in words of unusual tenderness, or give them too vivid marks of affection, for fear of awakening in their hearts a sentiment of passionate friendship for her.

Still less did Gertrude attach herself to those innumerable objects cupidity pursues, and whose possession enchaining the heart by a thousand bonds, arrests its flight, towards God. The faithful Spouse of Jesus wished nothing in her cell but what was indispensable. As soon as an object ceased to be necessary, she would not keep it a day longer, but obtaining permission, she gave it to another, without the slightest regard for her own natural sympathies or aversions.

So great was her delicacy of conscience, alarmed at the shadow of evil, so great the care she took to preserve her heart from sin and the solicitude with which she purified it from even the least stains, that Jesus Himself had often to console His Spouse, by showing her that these faults she deplored became for Him an occasion of joy.

Examining her conscience one sleepless night, she reproached herself bitterly for the habit she had contracted of saying these two words: God knows—*Deus scit;* and she conjured our Lord to pardon the past, and help her correct the future. "Ah! then," said Jesus, "wilt thou deprive Me of the pleasure thou givest Me, every time that falling into this fault thou dost humble thyself, and make a resolution of amendment? Is not a king pleased when he sees one of his soldiers struggling bravely against the enemies of the kingdom? Such is My satisfaction in this; and thou dost also increase thy merits."

But at the same time that His love encouraged and consoled her, Jesus excited her by a salutary fear to nourish in her heart horror for the least faults.

One day, whilst reciting the Canonical Hours, Gertrude heard the demon repeat after her in a hurried, excited manner a verse of a Psalm, and then say: "It is all pure loss indeed that your Creator, your Saviour and Beloved has given you organs so delicate that you can both speak rapidly and clearly articulate the words; for in one Psalm alone, you have mispronounced so many words, syllables, letters." "I understood from this," said Gertrude, "with what rigor the demon will accuse, at God's tribunal, those who precipitately recite the Divine Office."

"Alas!" said Gertrude one day, to Jesus Christ, "although my soul through Thy grace, appears to me now purified from its stains, I have reason to fear that it will soon be profaned by new ones. O dearest of Masters, teach me how I can quickly wash away my daily transgressions." "I do not wish thee ever to leave these stains on thy soul," replied our Lord, "and I will teach thee how to efface them. Hasten as soon as thou perceivest them, to address Me with all humility and devotion in the words of the Psalm, *Miserere me, Deus, secundum magnam tuam*, or, better perhaps, in the following invocation: 'O my Only Salvation, Jesus Christ, blot out all my sins by Thy holy death.'"

III.

A stranger to sin, free from all disorderly affection for creatures, Gertrude's heart sought God alone and found Him everywhere. To please Jesus in all things was the one aim of her life.

Our Lord Himself made this known to Saint Mechtilde by the following vision. He appeared to her seated upon an elevated throne, before which Gertrude came and went in various directions, but always with her face fixed upon His. "See," said He, "the life of Gertrude. She walks ever in My presence, never losing sight of Me for an instant; she has but one desire, that of knowing the good pleasure of My Heart, which when learned, she executes with incredible eagerness. Scarcely has she accomplished one of Its behests ere she applies to Me for others, which are executed with like celerity. And thus her whole life is devoted to My honor and glory." "But," asked Mechtilde, "how is it with gaze ever fixed on Thee, she sees so well all the faults and failings of the Sisters under her charge, and why does she attach so much importance to their least defects?" "Having a horror of seeing the least stains on her own soul, neither can she suffer them in the souls of those who are dear to her," replied our Lord.

Gertrude lived for Jesus Christ alone, and her fidelity lay at His feet every act of her life, with a simplicity we can but admire. If she preferred the books of her cell, the table upon which she wrote, it was because they served her better than anything else in making Jesus Christ known and loved. She even had an especial fondness for a certain book, after a Sister once said to her, "This book has done my soul much good."

Indeed, forgetting herself to see only Jesus therein, she considered as done for Him any kindness to herself, His Spouse, and even rejoiced at some little expense with which her infirmities had charged the monastery. It was to Him she referred the nourishment, rest, sleep, her body demanded. These words of His in the Gospel: "Whatsoever ye do to the least of these, is done to Myself," were to her an ever-burning beacon. One little incident alone which we give below, will prove how agreeable to Jesus Christ was this uprightness, this simplicity of Gertrude's heart:

Holy meditations had banished sleep from her eyes. Overcome by weariness and feeling very faint, Gertrude ate, in the middle of the night, a bunch of grapes, proposing to herself in so doing, the laudable intention of refreshing Jesus Christ thereby. "Now," said our Lord to her, "do I imbibe from thy heart a delicious beverage, whose sweetness compensates Me for the bitterness of the vinegar and gall, that My love of thee made Me taste on Calvary."

Gertrude had thrown the grape-skins and seeds upon the floor of her cell. She saw the demon attempt to pick up one of the skins, so as to produce it against her, at the tribunal of God, as a witness that she had broken the rule by eating before

Matins. But no sooner had he touched it, than she saw that it burnt his fingers, and he fled precipitately, uttering most frightful cries. Gertrude also noticed that in fleeing he was careful to avoid the burning skins and seeds.

IV.

Jesus encouraged Gertrude's fidelity by other lessons of charity. He told her of the jealousy of His love for her.

Grieved one day by the ingratitude and contempt with which a soul requited all her efforts to save it, she had recourse to Jesus. "It is I," said our amiable Lord, "Who have permitted thee to be thus afflicted. I desire that thou find neither consolation nor unalloyed joy in thy friends, that thus repelled, thou art constrained to come to Me and remain near Me. When a mother so loves a little child, that she longs to have it ever beside her, if it attempts to stray off to mingle in the sports of other children, does she not strive to recall it by speaking of apparitions or monsters it may meet, or even, perhaps, by placing in its way something that will frighten it? And thus do I act with thee, so as to keep thee ever near Me."

These confidences of the love of Jesus did not permit Gertrude to take pleasure in vain conversations. On the contrary, these wearied her, and just as soon as charity allowed her to withdraw, she would hasten to be more closely united to Jesus, either in solitude or meditation. Kneeling before a crucifix, she would address Him thus: "Master, behold me at Thy Feet. The conversation of creatures is weariness to my soul, which takes no pleasure but in Thy company. I turn away from them and come to Thee, O Sovereign Good, O Sole Joy of my heart."

Then, affectionately kissing on her crucifix the Five Wounds of Jesus, she would say at each: "I salute Thee, Jesus, Spouse ornamented with wounds as with flowers; I salute and embrace Thee, with a love in which all other loves are united; with the complacency of Thy Divinity itself, I kiss Thy Wound of love."

Gertrude had been practising this pious exercise a long time, when one day our Lord said to her: "Every time thou actest thus, I ponder in My Heart the five-fold return I will make thee in Heaven for the joy thou givest Me during thy sojourn on earth."

Simplicity and purity of intention are but aspects of, or acts springing from, purity of heart, which, when perfect, produces liberty. A friend of our Saint once asked Jesus Christ, at meditation: "What disposition of Gertrude's soul is it that pleases Thee most?" "Her liberty of heart," answered Jesus. "She permits her heart to be attached to nothing that may turn it aside from Me; hence, the progress she makes in the paths of sanctity. It is this liberty of heart which daily renders perfect her charity."

CHAPTER VIII.

The Confiding Love of Gertrude's Heart.

ALL the Saints have loved Jesus Christ: love of Jesus Christ is the perfection of sanctity; but this love presents different characteristics in the hearts of different Saints. The most salient feature in Gertrude's was her confidence. More fully than any other does she seem to have understood these words of Jesus: "Be of good heart, It is I, fear ye not."

I.

"All that I have received," she used to say, "I owe to my confidence in the gratuitous bounty of my God." Our Lord Himself, once reproaching a holy soul for the timidity of her petitions, said: "Why art thou not like My beloved Gertrude? There is nothing she does not hope for from My bounty, and there is nothing My bounty will ever refuse her."

In all things she had recourse to Jesus as a child to its mother, nothing, in her eyes, being too trivial to be recommended to Him. On one occasion, having lost a needle in a pile of straw, she besought Him to find it for her. "O dear Jesus," said she, "vainly, indeed, would I search for this needle; it were lost time; please get it for me Thyself." Extending one hand, and turning away her head, she immediately found the needle between her fingers.

She called Jesus by titles the most affectionate, and His brotherly Heart encouraged this confidence so dear to It. "I salute Thee, most loving Lord," said Gertrude to Jesus one day, "I who am but a vile little creature." "And I," immediately replied Jesus, "salute thee, My beloved

Spouse." Our Lord made her understand, on this occasion, that His Heart was most responsive to such tender epithets as Beloved, sweetest Jesus, and others of similar nature when dictated by piety and devotion.

Her confidence in Jesus banished all fear of death. One day, climbing up a rough place, Gertrude fell. On arising, she said, gaily: "O what a happiness, dear Jesus, had this fall but brought me to Thee!" "What!" exclaimed in astonishment those who were with her, "would you not be afraid to die without the Last Sacraments?" "I desire with all my heart to receive them," was her answer, "but I prefer to the Sacraments, Providence and my Master's Will. Moreover, whether I die suddenly or otherwise, I feel confident that His mercy will never be wanting."

II.

The contemporary author of Gertrude's life mentions especially as one of her most admirable acts of confidence in Jesus Christ, the frequency of her Communions, and the care she took to banish all exaggerated fears and false ideas of respect that might have kept her from the Eucharistic Table. Nothing she heard or read about the risk of making bad Communions, could ever have sufficient weight with her to make her forego even one. Such books or discourses, on the contrary, only animated her confidence in the infinite goodness of our Lord, and she would go to Communion without fear, endeavoring to inspire others with this same unwavering confidence.

"Humility," she would say to them, "should force you to communicate. What indeed were your longest, most assiduous preparations for Communion when you think of the grandeur of this Gift of Jesus Christ, wholly gratuitous? Even your greatest efforts would be but as a drop of water compared to the ocean. Of course, make all preparation in your power, but if it seem to you insufficient, walk fearlessly to the Holy Table, relying upon the bounty of Jesus."

Often Gertrude used her authority as Superior to lead to the Holy Table the Sisters who were too scrupulous.

One day, as she was quite worried on this account, thinking she had exceeded her limits and been wanting in discretion, our Lord said to her: "Fear not; thou hast done well. For thy consolation and guidance in future, I promise thee that, never shall thy counsels or orders be the occasion of an unworthy Communion. I will extend a loving welcome to all souls whom thou shalt bring to Me."

We meet throughout Gertrude's writings similar anecdotes, showing how agreeable to Jesus was her confidence. Let us recount a few of them. The reader will find therein abundant justification of the doctrine of the Saints and great theologians, which teaches that Communion may be allowed all Christians in a state of grace; that exemption from mortal sin suffices to render the Communion profitable; and humility and confidence supply the place of dispositions apparently more perfect—in a word, that the Holy Communion is the remedy of sinners, the nourishment of the weak, not the recompense of the Saints.*

Once when about to communicate, Gertrude said to Jesus, "Lord, what wilt Thou give me?" "I will give thee Myself, as I did to My Mother," was the answer. "Yes-

---

*Some directors oppose to souls who would communicate frequently, the following words of St. Francis de Sales: "To communicate every eight days, one should be free from mortal sin, likewise, all affection to venial sin, and have a great desire of communicating." These sentiments of St. Francis de Sales, which he, by a common error of his times, attributed to St. Augustine, are in reality, taken from the writings of Gennadius. A Saint, Alphonsus Liguori, whose authority, more especially on such points as these, is no less weighty than that of the Bishop of Geneva, writes as follows, about the end of the last century: "If the Blessed Francis de Sales, who advocated frequent Communion, had known that the above quoted passage was to be attributable not to St. Augustine, but to Gennadius, his (St. Augustine's) adversary, he

terday the Sisters received Thee with me; to-day, they do not. Shall my merits or recompense thereby be greater than theirs?" she asked. "In the world," answered Jesus, "the governor who is twice elected to his high office, takes precedence of him who occupies it but once; and shall not then one be more glorious in Heaven, the oftener he shall have received Me upon earth?" "Oh!" exclaimed Gertrude," what

would, no doubt, have given it slight consideration."
—St. Thomas of Aquin also attributed this same text to St. Augustine, but he (St. Thomas) excludes from the Holy Table only such as carry to it mortal sin already committed, or the *will* to commit *a mortal sin*; for it is thus he interprets the words of Gennadius: *Si mens in affectu* peccandi *non sit.*—Here are the words of St. Thomas (in 1 ad Cor. 2, lect. 7): "*Tertio modo dicitur aliquis indignus, ex eo quod cum voluntate peccandi mortaliter accedit ad Eucharistiam: inde, in libro de Dogmat. Eccles. dicitur: Si mens in affectu peccandi non sit.*"

How, moreover, the above quoted words of St. Francis de Sales may be reconciled with the doctrine universally admitted, St. Thomas formulates in these terms: "The presence of venial sins in the

then will be the glory of priests, since they communicate every day!" "Their glory is great indeed," answered Jesus, "if they communicate worthily. The Holy Communion, though always conferring glory, does not always, however, produce sensible joy. He who communicates from habit does not taste the sweetness of the Eucharist; whilst he who prepares his heart for Its reception by exercises of piety and soul is an obstacle to the impressions of sensible devotion which the Sacrament ordinarily produces; but it does not prevent the increase of sanctifying grace or charity, which is the principal fruit of the Sacrament."

In fine, directors are always careful to bear in mind that frequent falls into certain mortal sins are oftenest arrested, or diminished in their violence, only by very frequent Communions—such is the opinion, among others, of St. Ligouri, Cardinal Tolet and Cardinal de Lugo, three theologians of the first order.

Says Blessed Albert le Grand, it is not more natural for water to quench thirst, than it is for the Sacrament of the Altar to moderate the ardor of concupiscence.

devotion, tastes of this sweetness in proportion to his dispositions. In fine, he who approaches Me with fear and reverence, is less eagerly welcomed than he who comes to Me from love."

"Thou hast so often given me Thy Divine Heart, O my Beloved, what shall I gain in receiving Thee to-day, once more?" Thus spoke Gertrude after one of her Communions. Jesus answered: "Catholic Faith teaches that in communicating but once, the Christian receives Me, for his salvation, with all My goods—that is, with the united treasures of My Divinity and Humanity; but he does not appropriate the abundance of these treasures except by repeated Communions. At each new Communion, I increase, I multiply the riches which are to make his happiness in Heaven."

Among the directors of the monastery, was one whose sentiments on the subject of Communion were inspired more by zeal for justice than the spirit of mercy. And according to his ideas, some of the Sisters had not the requisite devotion for frequent Communion, or did not sufficiently prepare themselves for It. Expressing himself thus in a public instruction, he soon succeeded in breaking down the confidence of many of the Religious. Gertrude, greatly afflicted at this, and praying one day for the austere director, asked Jesus: "Lord, what dost Thou think of his conduct?" And our Lord answered:

"My delights are to be with the children of men. To satisfy My love I instituted this Sacrament. I remain thus with them until the end of the world, and I desire that they receive Me frequently. If then, any one, either by public instruction or private counsel, keep from the Holy Table a soul *not in mortal sin*, he hinders or interrupts the delights of My Heart. Did a young prince take great pleasure in talking to or recreating with children of an humble condition, would he not be vexed and irritated, were his preceptor harshly to reprove him and drive the children off, under the plea that it was unbecoming the dignity of a prince to indulge in such sports and associate with his inferiors."

"Lord," continued our Saint, "if the person of whom we have been talking were to change his sentiment and conduct on this point, wouldst Thou not pardon him all the wrong he has thereby done Thee to this day?" "Not only would I pardon him," answered Jesus, "but I would also be as delighted with him as the young prince with his preceptor, should the latter, relaxing his austerity, himself invite the children he had driven away, to return and resume their sports with his royal charge."

On one occasion, when the time of Communion had arrived, Gertrude felt less devotion than usual. "O my soul," she cried within herself, "behold thy Spouse comes to thee and thou art without adornment. But place all thy confidence in Him. Didst thou spend a thousand years in preparing thyself for His reception, thou wouldst still be unworthy of such a favor;

nothing thou couldst do would render thee worthy; come then to Jesus with humility and confidence." And as she thus advanced to the Holy Table, deeply impressed with the sense of her unworthiness, Jesus Himself came to her assistance, and arrayed her in His own virtues—His innocence, the humility which inclined Him towards us, His desire of being united to us, His love, the joy He tastes in our Communions, the confidence that urges Him to deliver Himself to us, and seek the delights of His Heart amid our lowliness and miseries—all of which adornments of the soul in its Spouse's eyes were shown to her under the figure of costly garments of various colors.

Once, after she had heard a long and terrible sermon upon God's holiness and justice, and the great fear with which one should approach the Sacraments, Jesus said to her: "It is not My justice, but My goodness and tenderness especially, I strive to manifest in the Eucharist. To be convinced of this, let one but consider how I am imprisoned in a little ciborium, and under what lowly appearances I come to men, I, the King of glory! Even thus is My justice imprisoned by My mercy, sweet mercy, which alone I extend to all in this Sacrament. Dost thou not see that whilst reducing Myself (in a certain sense) to the tiny proportions of the Host, I really subordinate My Body thus humiliated, to the body of him who receives Me? and this is only an image of my subjection of will to that of the communicant.

"Why not ponder the lesson given by the spectacle of the priest administering Holy Communion? He is clothed in rich sacred vestments, but he holds My Body in his naked hand, from which we may learn that although one should make every preparation for Communion by prayer, fasts, vigils and other exercises of piety, yet my compassionate tenderness brings Me nearer those who, naked of these ornaments, seek in this Sacrament only the fountains of My mercy, deeply conscious of their indigence and frailty. Such is My benignity, but many there are who will not believe it." On one occasion, the hour for Communion approached, and Gertrude had made no immediate preparation. "Alas! dear Jesus," said she, "Thou seest how unprepared I am to receive Thee! Since Thou canst do it, why hast Thou not supplied my deficiency?" "Does not a spouse," He answered, "sometimes prefer to see the white, delicate hand of His beloved unadorned by a glove? Even so, am I often more pleased with the humility of the communicant than his devotion."

Jesus does not even approve always of one's abstaining from Communion, for fear of scandalizing the witnesses of a fault recently committed.

A Sister in Gertrude's Community once absented herself from the Holy Table for this reason. As Gertrude was praying for her, our Lord enlightened her (Gertrude) as follows: "That fault was of service to our Sister's soul, because her humiliation and confession effaced not only it, but several others, even as in washing one stain off our hands we wash off any others that may be on them; and she ought to have communicated, satisfied that I had restored her soul its interior beauty, and striving to become indifferent to its exterior, that is, as to what others would think in seeing her communicate so soon after her fault. In acting otherwise, she has attached more importance to the judgment of men than to privation of the grace of the Sacrament."

"The fruits of this Sacrament are immeasurable," said our Lord to Gertrude again. "It compensates for all spiritual losses and deficiencies, provided It be received in *a state of grace.* Yes, when urged by the vehemence of My love, I unite Myself by Holy Communion to a soul *not in mortal sin,* I fill it with treasures untold; and, at that moment, all the inhabitants of Heaven, earth and purgatory even, experience the wonderful effects of My goodness."

In all Gertrude's writings, amid the numberless sweet invitations of the Heart of Jesus urging men to seek Him in the Eucharist, we find but one passage breathing the spirit of severity. It refers to those who having permitted their tongue slanderous or immodest words, come to the Holy Table, ere expiating by Confession, the injury done these, His two dearest virtues — charity and purity. "These persons," said our Lord, "give Me a cruel welcome in Communion, not unlike that of a man who should greet the guest crossing his threshold, by letting fall upon his head a heavy beam or a shower of stones. I feel the outrage the moment My Body touches their tongue." On hearing this, Gertrude pierced to the heart with grief, exclaimed: "O cruel man! how canst thou treat thus, Him Who flies to thy soul with an excess of love to embrace and save it!"

III.

The Saints always united to the worship of the Eucharist great devotion to our Lord's Passion; and Gertrude lived ever in the presence of Jesus on Calvary, studying her crucifix assiduously, and pondering the love which had embraced such sufferings for us.

At the beginning of her conversion, she ardently desired to have a crucifix which she could honor according to her good pleasure; but later, she began to fear lest this exterior devotion prove prejudicial to her interior exercises. Jesus reassured her. "No," said He, "on the contrary, it is very agreeable to Me to see thee thus honoring the crucifix. It is always by an effect of divine grace that men's eyes meet the Image on the Cross, and never once do they rest upon It, but his soul is benefited."

One day, as Gertrude was affectionately holding her crucifix and kissing it, our

Lord said to her: "Every time one kisses the crucifix, or looks at it with devotion, the eye of God's mercy is fixed upon his soul. He should then listen within himself to these words of tenderness from Me: 'Behold how I, for love of thee, have been nailed upon a cross — naked, disfigured, covered with wounds, all My members violently distended; and My Heart is so enamored of thee, that were it necessary for thy salvation, I would joyfully undergo, for thee alone, all that I suffered for the whole human race.'"

Gertrude's eyes ever sought her crucifix, sorrowful memento of the love of Jesus; and at night, this "bundle of myrrh" (for so she called it) never left her hands. Not even this satisfied her devotion, and she consecrated the whole of every Friday to meditation on the Passion.

More than once, our Lord made known to her how agreeable this devotion was to Him. "Even though a soul be lacking in fervor, yet will I look upon her with much love, if she sometimes meditate upon My Passion. It is an exercise possessing a value in My eyes infinitely surpassing that of any other. Even a short meditation upon My Passion, is worth more than long and multiplied acts of piety that have no direct reference to My sufferings and death."

IV.

Devoted to the Eucharist and the Passion, Gertrude nevertheless concentrated all her love of Jesus Christ, all her acts of piety in a devotion eminently embodying the others—devotion to the Sacred Heart.

Jesus, indeed, is entire in His Heart, and it is there she found at their inexhaustible source, the gifts of His love, there she saw the abysses of His most cruel sufferings.

It was in 1674, Jesus confided to Blessed Margaret Mary the mission of proclaiming to the world the love and plaints of His Heart; but four centuries previously, had He already ordered Gertrude to write the book revealing the depths of His Heart. Henceforth, she was (this book confirming it forever) the confidante most intimate, the Evangelist dearest among the Spouses of the Heart of Jesus.

On the feast of St. John, Gertrude was shown the disciple whom Jesus loved, in glory incomparable. "Dearest Lord," said our Saint to Jesus Christ, "why dost Thou present me, me so unworthy, to Thy Beloved Disciple?" "Because I wish to establish between him and thee a holy friendship; henceforth, will he be in Heaven, thy faithful protector."

John now said to Gertrude, "Spouse of my Master, come let us repose our heads upon our dear Lord's bosom; in it are all the treasures of Heaven." And as they were thus reclining, Gertrude on the right, John on the left side of Jesus, the Beloved Disciple continued: "Here is the Holy of Holies, whither are attracted as towards their centre, everything on earth and in Heaven."

Confiding Love of Gertrude's Heart. 115

Meanwhile, the beatings of the Heart of Jesus ravished Gertrude's soul. "Beloved of the Lord," she asked St. John, "did not these harmonious pulsations, now filling my soul with joy, delight thine when at the Last Supper thou didst recline upon the Master's bosom?" "Yes, their sweetness penetrated to the depths of my being." "Whence comes it then that thou hast said so little about it in the Gospel?" "My ministry in those days of the early Church was limited to making known the Uncreated Word, the Eternal Son of the Father, only saying what would serve as fruitful meditation for man's intelligence, and not exhausting the riches of these divine treasures. To later days, the far future, was reserved the grace of hearing the eloquent voice of the throbbings of Jesus Christ's Heart. At this persuasive voice, the world grown old, will be rejuvenated, and arousing from its torpor, it will be inflamed with the fire of divine love."

The following from another portion of

Gertrude's book sounds like an echo of these pulsations of our Lord's Heart: "Ah! dearest Lord," exclaimed Gertrude, on seeing her companions hastening to the chapel to assist at a sermon, whilst she, sick and suffering, was unable to accompany them, "how I would love to hear the sermon!" "Wouldst thou have Me to preach thee a sermon, Beloved?" said our Lord. "Oh! joyfully indeed would I listen to Thee," answered Gertrude. Then Jesus inclining her soul towards His Heart, she immediately distinguished two harmonious pulsations. "One of these throbs," said Jesus, "works the sanctification of the just, the other, the salvation of sinners."

"The first is ever pleading with My Father, to appease His justice and open the fountains of His mercy. By this also do I speak to all the Saints, making excuses to them for sinners, with the indulgence and zeal of a good Brother, and urging them to intercede for these unhappy creatures, deaf to the voice of My love. This same throb is likewise the incessant appeal I mercifully address the sinner himself, with that inexpressible desire of seeing him return to Me, which never wearies of awaiting him.

"By the second throb, I ever repeat to My Father how much I congratulate Myself on having shed My Blood to redeem so many just, in whose hearts I find My delights. I invite the whole celestial court to admire with Me the life of these perfect souls, and return thanks to God for the blessings He has already bestowed upon them or has prepared for them hereafter. In fine, this throb of My Heart is the habitual and familiar conversation I have with the just, either to testify My love for them, or to reprove their faults and thus hourly and daily advance them in the paths of perfection.

"As no exterior occupation, no distraction of sight or sound ever interrupts the throbbings of the heart of man, even thus in the providential government of the Universe, will nothing to the end of ages ever arrest, or slacken for an instant, these two pulsations of My Heart."

CHAPTER IX.

The Abandonment of Gertrude's Heart to the Good Pleasure of Jesus.

GERTRUDE had great confidence in the love of Jesus Christ become Man for love of His brethren; and without forgetting that Jesus is God, she always remembered that He is Man. This confidence, as we have seen, banished fear from her soul; and yet more—it disposed her to receive with unfailing faith and serenity, whatever came from His fraternal hand, blessing Him alike under all circumstances, and blindly abandoning herself to the good pleasure of His Heart.

I.

It was to these dispositions she owed the joy that irradiated her countenance—

nothing troubled her, neither physical sufferings, nor persecutions, nor interior trials. Tribulation, indeed, seemed rather to increase her joy, for she firmly believed that the love of Jesus Christ directed all the events of life, and it could draw from all, tribulation especially, the soul's best aliment. Hence, she neither tasted nor wished to taste anything save the good pleasure of Jesus Christ, and her heart could conceive of no other motives of action, either of choosing, desiring, mourning or rejoicing, save in this same good pleasure.

One trifling incident alone, of frequent recurrence, manifested to Gertrude's Sisters this perfect abandonment of her will. When presented with clothing, furniture, fruits—divers objects, and given her choice among each, she would close her eyes, and reaching forth her hand, accept as from Jesus Himself, the first of these articles it met.

"I could not be irritated against Gertrude," said our Lord to Saint Mechtilde, "for she finds all My ways perfect; and amiable, all My dispositions in regard to herself, even the most painful. Wherefore, all her works please Me, and when some imperfections are mingled with them, My mercy excuses these human infirmities."

"Gertrude," said He again, "clings so closely to My Heart, and I have so cemented the bonds uniting us, that she has become one with Me. She lives in absolute dependence upon My will; the members of one's body being not less dependent upon the heart than Gertrude upon My will. As a man says only in thought to the hand, do this; to the eye, look; to the tongue, speak; to the foot, advance, and these members instantly obey, so Gertrude is to Me a hand, an eye, a tongue, obeying My least desires."

II.

Numberless and admirable were the lessons of Jesus Christ imprinting these perfect dispositions upon Gertrude's heart. By degrees, He made her understand that everything comes to the just from the hand of God; that sufferings and humiliations are of an incomparable price and the most precious gifts of His providence; likewise, that spiritual infirmities, temptations, even faults may become, through His grace, powerful instruments of sanctification. Jesus also made known to her that He hears His friends' prayers, even when He seems to neglect or repulse them; that in His sight, the intention alone is the merit of one's works, and that even good desires are accounted works. He revealed to her the sovereign perfection of complete abandonment to His good pleasure, and the joy of His Heart at seeing a soul blindly commit itself to the care of His providence and love.

Gertrude knew how to profit by these lights; she obeyed these impulses of grace, and her heart learned to sing hourly the hymn of abandonment, the hymn of the

Heart of Jesus Christ: "Yea, Father, for so it hath seemed good in Thy sight:" *Ita, Pater, quia sic fuit placitum ante te.*

"Would that My friends," said Jesus to His Spouse, "deemed Me less harsh. Let them do Me the justice of believing that if sometimes I oblige them to serve Me laboriously and at a sacrifice, it is for their good alone, and their supreme good. Oh! if instead of being irritated at their troubles or against their enemies, they would consider these but the instruments of My paternal bounty! The rod in the hand of a father correcting his son must needs obey the will of him who wields it; and the wicked are the rod with which I correct My children. I do so in love, for were not contradiction and correction necessary to cure their faults, or increase their eternal glory, never should a rough wind blow upon them. A right understanding of these things would fill them with pity for their enemies instead of indignation, for in purifying the good, these often stain themselves with grievous sins."

In these words of the *Salve Regina* "Turn thine eyes of mercy towards us," Gertrude was once begging Jesus to give her health. He answered with a smile: "It is when thou art sick in body or troubled in soul that Mine eyes of mercy are fixed upon thee. Didst thou not know this?"

Sad and disheartened, she said to Him: "What shall I do now to please Thee?" "Learn to suffer patiently," was the answer. "Lord, teach me," she said. Then Jesus, drawing her towards Him, as does the teacher a little child whom he is going to teach its letters, spoke to her as follows: "Know thou that the King has no friend more dear than he who most resembles him. And hence, the greater is My love for thee, the more thou strivest to become like Me by patient suffering. Think, too, how all the court honors the King's favorite, believing that a glorious recompense in Heaven, will crown thy daily sufferings here. Bethink thyself again, that a faithful friend always compassionates his friend's sufferings, and endeavors to assuage them by his caresses. What then mayest thou not expect in Heaven from the tenderness of My affection which carefully notes all thy pains and sorrows?"

The monastery being burdened with a heavy debt, Gertrude begged our Lord to send the trustees the means of paying it. Jesus smiled sweetly, and said: "And what will I gain by that?" "What wilt Thou gain, Lord?" she answered. "That the trustees serve Thee with less solicitude and more devotion." "But suppose I do not wish them to serve Me thus," said Jesus. "It is the intention which makes all the merit, either of solicitude or peace. Had I preferred being served in the peace of contemplation, I would have provided for it, by exempting redeemed humanity from the cares incident upon nourishment, lodging, clothing;

but I derive more profit from the labor of My friends."

Gertrude, at this moment, perceived, bending low before Jesus, a man who, arising with great effort, placed in our Lord's hands a piece of gold, in the centre of which gleamed a beautiful diamond. "If I had granted thy petition," continued Jesus, "the trustee could have given Me only the gold piece without the diamond, and his recompense would have been less in Heaven. To do My will amid peace and consolation is to give Me a gold piece; amid trials and cares, is to add to the gold piece a costly diamond."

Gertrude was once praying for a friend who had sustained a serious injury. "I will restore her the use of the afflicted member," said our Lord, "although she purchases a great reward by her sufferings." "How can our sufferings have so much merit?" inquired Gertrude, "for we take remedies to assuage them, and we would rid ourselves of them entirely, if possible."

"Yes," replied our Lord, "but what suffering remains after one has exhausted attempts at relief, will, if borne patiently for love of Me, work the sufferer incomparable glory; I myself sanctified it, when in My Agony in the Garden, I cried to My Father, 'My Father, if it be possible, let this chalice pass from Me.'" "But, Lord," again asked Gertrude, "would it not be more pleasing to Thee if, instead of resigning ourselves lovingly only to such sufferings as will not be assuaged, one patiently suffers all, without seeking alleviation?"

"That is the secret of My justice;" He answered, "according to the human conception of things, these two diverse sentiments are like two beautiful shades of color, perfectly distinct, and so beautiful, that it were impossible to decide between them." "Lord," continued Gertrude, "when I make known to the sick person the instructions Thou hast given me on this subject, deign, I pray Thee, to fill her with a sensible impression of joy."

"No;" answered our Lord, "If I did so, three of her virtues would lose their brightness—her patience, for the joy would make her forget her sufferings; her faith, these vivid impressions rendering evident the mysterious designs of My Providence; her humility, in the consciousness that I had thus favored her. It is far more profitable to her soul, that she believe God deems her unworthy of communicating His graces and benefits directly to her."

III.

Gertrude had arisen from several spells of illness; after a seventh relapse, she said to Jesus: "O Father of Mercies, will I be long sick?" "My Paternal Providence," answered Jesus, "sees fit to leave thee in ignorance of this. If I had told thee at the beginning of thy illness, that thou wert to suffer seven successive attacks, thy patience perhaps had not sufficed for such a burden; if I were to tell thee now that this spell would be the last, or of short duration, such knowledge would greatly diminish thy merits. Leave to Me the disposing of this as of everything else in thy regard; I know thy weakness, and I will proportion the trial according to thy strength. Thanks to the ingenuities of My love, thy will stands firmer after the seventh attack than at the first."

Some one complaining to Gertrude of a lack of divine consolations in her spiritual exercises and even in Holy Communion on solemn feast days, our Saint asked Jesus the reason. "It is for the greater good of her soul," He answered; "humility is often more profitable than devotion. Moreover, I am often nearest the soul at the very time it complains of My remoteness. When a friend embraces us, do we distinguish his features as clearly as when he is a little farther off? With consolation, are not unfrequently mingled imperfections that impede the abundant effusion of My graces. I could prevent these imperfections even whilst flooding the soul with sensible joy, but when humiliations ward them off, the soul acquires more merit."

A lay Sister was greatly troubled that the multiplicity of her manual labors interfered with her meditations. Gertrude recommended her to our Lord. "She wishes," answered Jesus, "to serve me an hour, and I exact much more of her, desiring to have her with Me the whole day, these multiplied duties of which she complains, uniting her inseparably to Me: wherefore, let her do all things, not only with an eye to the corporal welfare of the Sisters, but even the advancement of their souls in My love. Every time she performs an action thus, she prepares for Me a delicious repast."

Gertrude was once recommending to Jesus a person who often fell into the same faults. "I will leave her the temptation," said He; "it causes her to acknowledge and deplore the fault she tries so hard to correct, and yet has the humiliation of falling into so often. This nourishes humility in her heart; and whilst she combats the inclination and grieves over these sins, I am working within her the destruction of several others that she scarcely perceives. When we wash our hands to rid them of one stain, we also wash off others that may be on them."

Our Saint begging Jesus to correct the faults of one of the Superiors of the monastery, He made this reply: "Not he alone of whom thou speakest to Me has faults, but each of the other Superiors of My dear Community, has likewise, his own. It is My tender love for thee which has willed it thus for thy greater merit. It is indeed far more meritorious to obey a Superior whose defects are apparent, than one whose works seem perfect."

IV.

"I have been prayed for so much," said a person to Gertrude, "and yet I do not experience any of the good effects." Gertrude asked our Lord the reason of this. His answer was: "Ask that person if some one were to offer her either a benefice for her little brother, or its present value in money, which she would choose. Her good sense would no doubt prompt her to select the former, the revenues of which would accumulate until the child reached his majority, whilst money placed in his hands would soon be frittered away. Let her apply this to herself, and confide entirely in My bounty; I am her Father, her Brother, her Friend, much more preoccupied with her true interests, both of body and soul, than she could ever be with those of another. I faithfully collect the fruits of all the prayers, all the good desires offered Me for her, and I will remit them into her hands, at a time when it will be out of her power to let them slip from her."

Gertrude herself was once complaining thus to our Lord: "Thou hast said to me, dearest Lord, 'Command, and I will hasten to obey, even as a subject his sovereign.' I wish not, my good God, to doubt these, Thy words of merciful condescension, but whence comes it then, that so often my prayers seem without effect?" Jesus answered: "A queen says to her servant, 'Take that string off my left shoulder.' He hastens to obey, but perceives that it hangs from the right. Now, as the queen cannot see her shoulders, he quietly takes the string hanging from the right, and gives it to her, knowing that it is better to act thus than violently to snatch from the left side a string of some of her garments. And thus it is with thy prayers; when I seem not to hear them, I am often, in reality, obeying thy dearest desires, and according thee graces more precious than those thou askest."

V.

One festival day, Gertrude confined to her cell by sickness, grieved at not being able to assist at Vespers. "Alas! dear Lord Jesus," she said, "would it not be more to Thy glory were I now with my Sisters, chanting Thy praises, instead of losing my time like this in quiet and inaction?" Jesus answered: "Is not a spouse as well pleased to converse familiarly with his beloved at home as to behold her elsewhere, arrayed in fine and costly garments? Know, however, that good desires alone content Me, when it is I who hinder their execution, and nothing is as agreeable to Me as to have My friends abandon themselves to My good pleasure."

"What are thy commands, O My Sovereign Mistress?" said Jesus, on one occasion, to Gertrude. She answered: "I beg of Thee, with all my heart, to accomplish most perfectly in me, Thy good pleasure." Jesus then mentioned several persons whom Gertrude had recommended to Him, and continued: "What shall I do for these, and also that other, who was recommended to thy prayers to-day?" "I ask nothing, save that Thy most amiable will be accomplished in them." "And what for thyself?"

Abandonment of Gertrude's Heart. 135

"Only that Thou deign accomplish fully in me, and in every creature, Thy holy will, and to obtain this, I would undergo every torture." "This disposition of thy heart is so agreeable to Me," said Jesus, "that it has adorned thy soul with beauty incomparable, so that it now appears in My sight as if it had never contradicted My will even in things the most trifling."

As Gertrude was once praying for a person who had said in her presence: "The trials God sends me are not the sort I need; a different kind would suit me better," our Lord answered her thus: "Ask her what kind of trials she does need, for it is only through these she gains Heaven; tell her also that when they do come, she must bear them patiently." "Our Lord's tone and manner made Gertrude understand that it is very dangerous to desire crosses different from those He sends. Suddenly, changing His countenance and voice, He said to Gertrude: "Art thou, too, dissatisfied with the trials

I send thee? Do thine seem to thee ill chosen?" "Oh! no, Lord," was her answer; "I acknowledge, and will acknowledge all my days, that Thy Providence has wonderfully disposed every event of life—health or sickness, joy or sorrow, for the good of both my body and soul." It now seemed to Gertrude that Jesus conducted her, first to the Heavenly Father, then to the Holy Spirit, before whom, at our Lord's invitation, she repeated the profession she had just made, after which, Jesus said to her: "From this moment henceforward, I am obliged to have a more especial care of thee," by which she understood that Jesus encompasses with His Providence those who thus commit themselves to His love, as the Superior of a monastery feels his obligation to watch solicitously over the necessities of the Religious, since by their vows they have renounced all temporal goods and cares.

"The soul," continued Jesus, "who blindly confides in Me, is that dove mentioned in Scripture as chosen among thousands. She is that best beloved Spouse whose look alone wounds My Heart; and if I were powerless to help her, My Heart would experience such desolation as all the joys of Heaven could not assuage." "I see," answered Gertrude, "that abandonment to Thee ravishes Thy Heart. But tell me how to obtain this perfect gift of Thee?" "My grace," said Jesus, "is wanting to no one; and what person is there that cannot, if he will, at least force his lips to murmur some of those many words of abandonment and confidence scattered throughout the Holy Scriptures, such as: 'Thou hast saved my soul out of distresses;' 'Although He should slay me, I will trust Him?'"

"Some trials," continued Jesus, "are much harder to bear than others, and probe the human heart to its depths; for instance, the grief one feels at the death of a dear friend, or the hourly expectation of it. But in all such cases, the afflicted Christian, assisted by My grace, can resign himself to My good will and say: 'I accept whatever God ordains; and I would willingly sacrifice my own desires were I given a choice between them and the accomplishment of His will.' The soul thus forcing itself for even an hour to bend its will to Mine, may rest confident that I will ever ensure to this generous act its first perfection, and far from being offended by that prostration and dejection which naturally follows, I will make all conducive to its eternal welfare and temporal consolation. When wrapped in grief, this soul deplores its sad loss, and ponders the cruel void death has made in its affections, My compassion will regard this as a mere outgrowth of human frailty, and I engage myself to compensate these passing sorrows by never-ending joys and merit. My goodness will constrain Me to act thus. When the artist has made a place in the precious metal for its setting of pearls, he must needs insert them. Nor does My goodness ever leave its works unfinished."

CHAPTER X.

The Zeal of Gertrude's Heart.

THE peaceful abandonment of the Heart of Jesus to Its Father's good pleasure, was Its supreme act of zeal for His Father's glory; this abandonment, in reality, constituting the absolute reign of God over man's will. Jesus longed to establish this reign of God in all souls, thus saving them and extending God's kingdom, and the fire of zeal, which devoured His Sacred Heart, was also a burning flame in that of Gertrude's, His Spouse.

I.

It was zeal for the salvation of souls which urged her to reveal those wonderful graces with which our Lord favored her;

zeal, also, which made her so often defer her frugal repasts, abridge her hours of repose, neglect the care of her delicate body. Meditation was to her an anticipated Heaven, yet, whilst thus engaged, did a soul solicit her charity, she never hesitated an instant at the sacrifice, but abandoned her dearest exercises with a cheerfulness that beamed in her countenance.

Her meditations were, we might say, scarcely more than an incessant prayer to God for the increasing sanctification of the just and the conversion of sinners. Always patient, compassionate and affable towards those whose vices or faults stood between their souls and God, she nevertheless could not tolerate the vices and faults themselves, and spared herself no effort for their eradication. Some one once said to her: "Pray no longer for such or such persons; waste no more advice on them; if they are damned you will certainly have nothing to answer for." "Oh!" answered our Saint, "how these cruel words pierce me like a sword: I would rather die than console myself thus for the loss of a soul!"

One of the most habitual and deepest griefs of her heart, was the thought of so many Jews and pagans who lived, and died perhaps, without participating in the riches of the divine mercy.

II.

Gertrude prayed and immolated herself for the conversion of infidels and sinners; but the greatest activity of her zeal was directed to the sanctification of the souls of the Religious under her charge. Jesus, one day, appeared to her, almost bowed to the ground beneath the weight of an immense house upon His shoulders. "Thou seest," He said to her, "how nearly crushed I am beneath this edifice, which is that of the Religious State; it is everywhere giving way, and few are the generous souls that meet and assist Me in bearing the burden of it. O My Best Beloved, have compassion upon Me." From that day henceforth, Gertrude was most vigilant in maintaining the rule in her monastery, herself setting the example of a heroic fidelity in the observance of it. "Every Religious," said our Lord to Gertrude, "is obliged to labor for the correction and sanctification of his brethren. He should advise them of their faults, or acquaint the Superior with them, that they may be remedied. Let no one shirk this positive duty, excusing himself by saying: 'It is not my place to correct others,' or, 'I am no better than they are.' Such conduct is like that of Cain, whose answer to God's inquiry about his brother was: 'Am I my brother's keeper?' It is I who warn every Religious that if, through his negligence or indifference, his brethren perish, I will demand of him an account of these souls, more rigorous, perhaps, in some instances, than of the Superiors themselves; for circumstances may prevent these latter from remarking defects that others, in a different position, see readily. Not to labor to correct the faults of one's brethren is to be an accomplice; for it is written: not only 'Woe to him who does evil,' but likewise, 'Woe to him who consents to evil: *Væ facienti; væ, væ consentienti.*'"

To these words of Jesus deeply engraven upon Gertrude's heart, was due the penetrating vigor of her corrections. Without forgetting, for an instant, her maternal benignity, she could give, when needed, such vigor to her accents and words that the guilty trembled and the most rebellious hung the head.

Gertrude had once corrected thus a Sister whose many virtues rendered her very dear to our Saint. Shortly after, the Sister deeply touched, said to Jesus: "Lord, I pray Thee, temper this too fervent zeal of Thy beloved Gertrude." "When I lived on earth," He answered, "the sight of iniquity enkindled within Me just such zeal." "But, Lord," continued the Sister, "Thou didst say harsh words only to those who were obstinate in evil; whilst Gertrude is very severe to those who are esteemed Thy friends, and considered good." "Likewise did those among the Jews," replied our Lord, "who were most violent against Me, pass, in the eyes of all, for very holy persons."

It was thus Jesus urged and assisted His Spouse, to pursue even the shadow of evil in the souls of the just, at the same time that He revealed to her how great must be her hope in His mercy for the conversion of the greatest sinners—stimulating her zeal, in turns, by fear and love.

A clergyman having said in her presence, that no one could be saved without charity —that is, unless the repentance for his sins proceeded, in part, at least, from love of God, Gertrude felt grieved and perplexed. "Alas!" she thought, "what will become of so many sinners, who seem to repent at the hour of death, but only from fear of hell?" Jesus answered: "When I see on the brink of death, persons who have been not unkindly disposed towards Me, and who, perhaps, have done some good works in My honor, just at the moment they are about to leave this world, I appear to them, with looks so compassionate and loving, that their hearts are touched to the depths, and they make that act of contrition which saves their souls. I desire that My elect in remembering My other benefits, would render thanks to Me for this supreme act of mercy towards dying sinners."

CHAPTER XI.

The Gratitude of Gertrude's Heart.

JESUS, whilst revealing to Gertrude all the mysteries of His love for her and for sinners, frequently invited her to pay Him, in the name of all, a debt nearly all forget — that of thanksgiving. Gertrude was grateful, very grateful, and her life, her writings are one hymn of thanksgiving. Let the following from her book confirm our words:*

---

*Within the last few years, God seems to have awakened in the hearts of men a strong impulse of gratitude, three Associations or Works devoted to Thanksgiving having been recently founded, one in Spain, and two in France. The oldest of these, having St. Gertrude for its especial patroness, we deem it not out of place to give here a hasty glance at them:

The Gratitude of Gertrude's Heart. 147

"May my heart, my soul, my senses, return Thee thanks for Thy infinite mercies, O God most tender, Friend most faithful. Powerless to bless and thank Thee, as I should, O my God, I pray Thee to cover with Thy benefits, those who aid me, if only by a sigh, in paying Thee my

I. Schools of Gratitude (Escuelas de Gratitud). The founder of these is an old officer of high rank in the Spanish army. In these schools, abandoned children are collected. Here they are raised and educated gratuitously, the principal feature of their education being the development in their hearts of gratitude to God. The organization of the work is admirable. Thanks to God's all powerful aid, the noble Spanish soldier's work finds generous promoters in France. Spain already counts four Schools of Gratitude. The principal house is in Madrid, and was founded in 1863.

For more ample information, address *Sr. D. Manuel Campoy, Director de los Escuelas de Gratitud, Bajada de Sta. Cruz, Madrid, Spain.*

II. Association of Thanksgiving.—The centre of this Work is at Mauron, a little village of Morbihan. Its first Indulgences were accorded by Pius IX, November 19, 1859.

Feasts of the Association.—The Thirteenth Sun-

debt of gratitude. I henceforth offer **Thee** for them the Passion of Thy Beloved Son, and conjure Thee to keep alive in my heart to the end of ages this offering, that it may obtain full pardon of all their sins and negligences.

"Be Thou blessed, O my Lord most

day after Pentecost (this is the principal), Corpus Christi, the Sacred Heart, the Annunciation, the Visitation, the Chair of St. Peter at Rome, on all of which feasts may be gained a Plenary Indulgence; likewise, on the day of one's enrolment upon the register of the Association. There are also various partial Indulgences.

Practices of the Association.—A monthly Communion of thanksgiving, an offering of two Masses a year in thanksgiving, and daily aspirations of thanksgiving.

No one is received into the Association, except those who, after reflection, are determined seriously to offer acts of thanksgiving to God both for themselves and others, striving thus to pay the great debt of gratitude.

Further information may be obtained from *M. Levoyer, Priest, Director of the Association at Mauron, Morbihan.*

III. The Association of Perpetual Thanksgiving.

The Gratitude of Gertrude's Heart. 149

merciful, for the assurance of my hopes Thy bounty has given me by promising that, whoever returns Thee thanks for me, though he be in sin, shall not leave this world until Thou hast converted him, or guided him to greater sanctity, and his heart be worthy of becoming Thy abode."

—This was founded about the year 1853, although Providence had prepared the way for it several years previously. The principal centres are Rome, Marseilles, Bordeaux, etc. In Rome, the chapel of the Association is the Oratorio del Caravita; in Marseilles and Bordeaux, the chapel of the Jesuits.

End of the Association.—To offer the Holy Trinity Perpetual Thanksgiving for all blessings vouchsafed man, especially for the gift of the Holy Eucharist, the new manifestation Jesus has made to the world of the riches of His Divine Heart, for the Blessed Virgin's glorious privileges, and all the graces accorded the Church through the intercession of the Immaculate Mother of God.

Practices of the Association.—*Daily* to recite a short formula of thanksgiving.

Every Month to assist at a pious reunion on the third Thursday, at which reunion, a Mass of **Thanksgiving** is celebrated before the **Blessed**

For ages, pious souls have responded to Gertrude's prayers, and gathered the fruits of the divine promises, by reciting the following formula of thanksgiving:

O Gertrude, blessed Spouse of Jesus Christ, with all my heart do I thank Him for the gifts He has lavished upon thee!

Sacrament exposed. This is followed by a sermon on Thanksgiving, Benediction of the Blessed Sacrament and the singing of the *Magnificat*.

Once a year the members are invited to make *a week's thanksgiving,* offering up with this intention all their works, etc., of that week.

From Wednesday of Passion Week to Holy Thursday inclusive, the members make a Novena of Thanksgiving for the institution of the Blessed Eucharist, in which they also return thanks to God for all the favors and dignities vouchsafed priests, and solicit His bounty for worthy celebrants of the Mysteries of the Altar.

Feasts of the Association.—The feasts of the Epiphany, Pentecost, Corpus Christi, the Sacred Heart, Annunciation, Our Lady of Thanksgiving (April 12), the Seven Dolors (third Sunday in September), St. John the Evangelist, St. Gertrude, the principal patroness of the Association, and St. Felix of Cantalicio, secondary patron.

Thanks be to Jesus, that He eternally predestined thee for such favors!

Thanks be to Jesus, who didst so amorously draw thee to Him!

Thanks be to Jesus, who united thy heart to His!

Thanks be to Jesus, who prepared

Plenary Indulgences.—On all the above-mentioned feasts; on the third Thursday of each month, on the day of reunion; on any one day of the Week of Thanksgiving, also, on any one day of the Novena of Thanksgiving, and on the day of one's enrolment on the register of the Association.

Children who make the Week of Thanksgiving, but have not yet been admitted to the Holy Table, are entitled to the Plenary Indulgence, upon the performance of certain good works enjoined by their confessor.

The Association enjoys also several partial Indulgences. It is recommended to the associates that they frequently make use of this short and beautiful aspiration: "*Deo gratias!*"

The directors of this Association published, in 1864, a pamphlet of two hundred pages, and entitled, *De L'Action De Grace. Victor Palmé, Paris, Rue Saint Sulpice,* 22.

A Religious Community, that of *Notre Dame*

for Himself in thy heart a delightful abode!

Thanks be to Jesus, who consummated the work of thy sanctity, crowning thee worthily in Heaven!

O happy Spouse of Jesus, I congratulate thee, and beg of thee to obtain for me,

Auxiliatrice, lauded and blessed by Pius IX, is the centre of this Association.

The principal work of this Community, combining both the active and contemplative life, is the preservation in the paths of virtue and piety of young workingmen, apprentices, those who stand in city stores, etc., and the most salient feature of their Institute is the cultivation among themselves and those under their charge, of the spirit of gratitude and thanksgiving. Their houses could justly be called Houses of Our Lady of Thanksgiving, for they are indeed both asylums of preservation and schools of thanksgiving.

The Heart of Jesus in the Eucharist, is the principal object of their worship of thanksgiving, these Religious of *Notre Dame Auxiliatrice*, day and night, in the name of their brethren, responding, by uninterrupted thanksgivings, to this plaint of Jesus: "*Instead of gratitude, they have for Me only ingratitude.*"

through the gentle Heart of thy Spouse, a heart pure, humble, gentle, full of confidence, burning with love for the Heart of Jesus and filial devotion to His glorious Mother—a heart, in fine, devoured with zeal for God's glory and the salvation of souls. Amen.

These two aims, so beautiful and opportune, of this Institute, and the efficacious means employed to attain them, have greatly rejoiced the Holy Father, and his benedictions have rapidly produced abundant fruits, so that it already has four houses in France:

At Toulouse, Rue des Buchers, 4;
At Castelnauday, Faubourg Montléon;
At Amiens, Rue des Coiroyers, 105;
At Lyons, Rue François Dauphin, 7.

CHAPTER XII.

Gertrude's Blessed Death.

FORTY years and eleven days had Gertrude filled the office of Abbess,* when she was struck by paralysis, which affected almost her whole body, leaving her in this helpless condition twenty-two weeks. During all this time she could say but these two words: "*Spiritus meus*, my spirit." The Sisters who waited on her, most frequently were unable to understand her desires, for in spite of all her repeated efforts, she could not interpret them by

---

*According to several authors, Gertrude first entered the monastery of Rodersdorff, of which she was elected Abbess, at the age of thirty. Thence she went to Heldelfs, which she governed until her death. Heldelfs is about half a mile distant from Eisleben, Gertrude's native place.

anything more intelligible, murmuring again and again, "*Spiritus meus.*" When, as often happened, after continued repetitions of them, her attendants could not make out what she desired, our amiable Saint would smile so sweetly and graciously that they smiled too, and she would relapse into silence, and this without the slightest sign of impatience, her countenance retaining even to the last such unruffled serenity, her eyes such untroubled peace, that it was truly remarked of her, "Gertrude's eyes are those of a dove."

When the Sisters or others came into her cell, Gertrude would greet them with a look and a slight movement of the hand paralysis had spared. Then she remained motionless in an unbroken peace, which was communicated to her visitors, and filled them with so vivid an impression of joy that no one ever grew weary of watching beside her.

On learning that one of her Religious was seriously ill, she made known her desire of being taken to the sick one's bedside by such expressive and earnest gestures that no one could resist them. Reaching the spot, she testified her compassion by tender maternal caresses, and left her spiritual daughter consoled.

When the hour of Gertrude's summons to life eternal had come, one of the Sisters (she to whom Gertrude had dictated the Book of the Insinuations) saw Jesus draw nigh his Spouse. Joy irradiated His Face. On His right, was the Blessed Virgin, on the left, the beloved Disciple, St. John, whilst surrounding them was a multitude of Angels, Virgins and other Saints. The Virgins especially were most numerous, and the monastery seemed filled with them.

The Sisters were reading beside her bed the account of the Passion. When they came to these words: "And bowing His Head, He gave up the ghost," Jesus leaned over Gertrude, and with His two hands, opening His own Heart, He transfused the flames into her soul.

The Community continuing the prayers, said to Him: "Console her, Lord, as Thou didst Thy Blessed Mother at the hour of her holy death." Then Jesus, turning to His Mother, addressed her thus: "O My Sovereign, My Mother, tell Me the consolation I then gave thee, that I may communicate it to My Beloved." "My sweetest consolation was the assured refuge of Thine arms." And Jesus now promised that this consolation should also be Gertrude's.

Her agony lasted the whole day; all which time our Lord never left her side, whilst the Angels came and went, singing around her in ravishing accents of melody, "Come, come, come, O Queen, the delights of Paradise await thee. Alleluia! Alleluia!"

The moment which was to cut asunder the bonds of the flesh approached. Jesus said to her: "At last, I may give thy soul the kiss of peace, which is to unite it to

Me; at last, My Heart may present thee to My Heavenly Father."

And, at that instant, Gertrude's blessed soul, escaping from its earthly tabernacle, rose towards Jesus, and penetrated the sanctuary of His Sacred Heart.*

Her holy remains were exposed in the monastery chapel. Next day, at the hour of their sepulture, our Saint's confidante saw a multitude of souls, delivered from the flames of Purgatory, through Gertrude's intercession, join her in Heaven.

The Religious of the monastery of Heldelfs were inconsolable at Gertrude's departure. "Never," says her biographer, "was any one more loved than she. The young girls who had been educated at the abbey, even children, some of whom were scarcely seven years of age—all seemed to cling more closely to her than to their own

* Father Laurent Clement fixes the date of Gertrude's death on the 17th of November, 1292. Gertrude was then seventy years of age.

Gertrude's Blessed Death. 159

mothers, and long days after she was laid in the tomb, their tears were still undried."

God consoled her weeping friends by several celestial communications: a Sister saw her standing before God's throne. "O Sovereign Benefactor," murmured Gertrude, "I ask a favor of Thy bounty—every time my daughters visit my grave, assuage their grief and allay their temptations, that it may be to them a sign by which they will recognize that I am indeed their mother."

Another day, one saw her prostrate before God's throne praying for her daughters. Jesus answered her: "The eyes of My mercy shall be ever fixed upon them."

Deign, O glorious and amiable Saint, to adopt as thy children, all who, having read this brief sketch of thy life, shall thank the Heart of Jesus for having so loved thee; guide their souls, and direct towards them the merciful glances of the Blessed Virgin

Mary; and obtain through her powerful intercession that the Heart of Jesus in these our days, deluge the world with such waves of grace as will purify it of its crimes, and renew its youth to the greater glory of God! Amen.

CONTENTS.

	PAGE.
Introductory,	5

CHAP.
I.—Gertrude's Childhood,	17
II.—Gertrude's Conversion,	21
III.—Gertrude's Sanctification,	29
IV.—The Share the Blessed Virgin had in Gertrude's Conversion,	43
V.—The Humility of Gertrude's Heart,	59
VI.—The Benignity of Gertrude's Heart,	73
VII.—The Purity of Gertrude's Heart,	83
VIII.—The Confiding Love of Gertrude's Heart,	95
IX.—The Abandonment of Gertrude's Heart to the Good Pleasure of Jesus,	119
X.—The Zeal of Gertrude's Heart,	139
XI.—The Gratitude of Gertrude's Heart,	146
XII.—Gertrude's Blessed Death,	154

www.ingramcontent.com/pod-product-compliance
Lightning Source LLC
Chambersburg PA
CBHW030259170426
43202CB00009B/808